REFRESH OF A FAVORITE

BASIC GUIDE
TO ROTARY CUT QUILTS

DEDICATION

To beginning quilters everywhere.
(Remember, every expert quilter was once a beginner.)

2007 by Leisure Arts, Inc.,
701 Ranch Drive, Little Rock, AR 72223

Welcome to the pleasures of patchwork! We love making quilts for our homes--wall quilts, baby quilts, bed-sized quilts--and we know you will too. It's "sew" much fun.

If you've never made a quilt before--this book is for you. We have geared it to help you get started with quick rotary cutting methods, easy machine sewing, and speedy quilting techniques to make your first quilt, and, hopefully, many more.

Included in our Getting Started section are tips on buying fabric and acquiring the basic tools you need to begin. We also tell you how to set up your sewing machine for accurate stitching results. Nine Patchwork Lessons teach you how to make the nine blocks used in the projects pictured in the book. We've included step-by-step photos and illustrations to make learning as easy as possible. Making Your Quilt A Quilt tells you how to turn your patchwork into a real quilt by layering it with batting and backing, quilting it, and finishing the edges.

Piecing patchwork quilts used to involve meticulous tracing around templates and hours of laborious cutting with scissors. Not any more! The methods we've used in this book--rotary cutting, making strip sets, stitching "diagonal seams," machine piecing, and machine quilting--are used by modern quilters everywhere to make quilts quickly to decorate their homes and keep their loved ones warm.

Again, welcome to patchwork! We hope you love it as much as we do.

Marianne and Liz

table of

contents

GETTING STARTED

BASIC TOOLS FOR YOUR SEWING KIT

Quilters love gadgets and supplies, and quilt shops always seem to have new tools. We've limited this list to just the items you need to get the projects in this book started. In the Making Your Quilt a Quilt section, you'll find a short list of additional supplies you'll need to finish your project.

CUTTING TOOLS
Rotary Cutter
Many brands are available. We prefer the large (45mm-diameter) or extra large (60mm-diameter) cutter. We like to cut several thicknesses of fabric at a time, and the larger cutters do a better job of this. It's a good idea to buy a package of replacement blades when you buy your cutter.

Cutting Mat
An 18" x 24" mat is adequate for your rotary cutting. Most boards come with a printed grid on one side. Gridded or non-grid is fine.

Rulers
Choose rulers that are marked in ⅛" increments and have guidelines for cutting 45° angles. We favor the Omnigrid® brand for accuracy and the easy visibility of yellow markings. The three ruler sizes we just can't do without are: a 6" x 12" for cutting strips across the fabric width and for cutting segments from strips and strip sets; a 6" x 24" for making long cuts, and a 15" ruled square for straightening the end of fabric before cutting strips, cutting setting pieces, checking blocks for size accuracy, and squaring off corners before sewing on binding.

Scissors
You'll need a small pair of scissors for snipping threads and clipping corners. We like Fiskars® brand children's school scissors—they are inexpensive, brightly colored and thus easy to find, and their blunt ends make them safer.

SEWING SUPPLIES
Sewing Machine
A good quality sewing machine in excellent working order is essential for successful patchwork. A simple straight-stitch sewing machine is all you need. If your machine has been in a closet for over a decade, take it to a repair shop to be serviced. Have the tension checked and adjusted and the machine cleaned and oiled. If you don't have a ¼" wide presser foot (sometimes called a "patchwork foot"), the repair shop can order one to fit your machine. Have a size 80/12 needle installed and purchase several packages of needles. Sewing machine experts recommend putting in a new needle every six hours of sewing.

Thread
Use 100% cotton or cotton-covered polyester thread for machine patchwork. Medium gray is a good color to use for sewing patchwork since it blends with most fabrics. Stay away from 100% polyester thread—it's too strong and can cut cotton fibers.

Pins, Pincushion, Needles, Thimble
Choose long, thin, rustproof dressmaker's pins with small glass heads. We like magnetic pin holders, but an old-fashioned cloth tomato pin cushion will work fine. For hand quilting and for finishing binding, purchase a package of assorted needles called "betweens." Choose an inexpensive thimble that fits the middle finger of your sewing hand. We also like the new "thimble pads," which are leather dots with a sticky back.

LIZ SAYS:
It's important always to use a sharp blade for accurate rotary cutting, so always have replacements on hand.

MARIANNE SAYS:
Unfortunately, you will also need a seam ripper. We've been sewing for over two decades, and we still have to "un-sew" seams on occasion!

LIZ SAYS:
Keeping your sewing machine in good working order and replacing needles frequently will make your patchwork life happier

Measuring Tape

Buy a 120"-long tape instead of the standard 60" one. The longer tape is great for measuring quilt borders.

Iron and Ironing Board

You will need an iron with both steam and dry settings.

FABRICS FOR QUILTS

We prefer 100% cotton broadcloth-weight fabric for quilts. It's easy to sew, neither too stretchy nor too tightly woven, doesn't ravel easily, washes well, and is relatively colorfast. If you buy your fabric in a quilt shop, this is probably the only kind of fabric they stock. If you shop at a larger fabric store, you will probably find a section with fabric suitable for quilts. Check the end of the bolt to make sure the fabric content is 100% cotton.

Choosing Fabrics

When we shop for fabric, we put different combinations of bolts together on a large table. Then we step back and look at the overall mix of values and visual textures. If one fabric looks out of place, we replace it with another.

Sometimes we purchase just ¼ yard of each fabric to make a sample block and actually test our fabric combination before purchasing all of the fabric for the quilt.

Employees of quilt shops and fabric stores are usually glad to assist you in selecting fabrics. Some shops and mail-order sources offer "starter packs" of coordinating fabrics, often in ¼-yard or ½-yard cuts. Buying packs is an easy way to increase the variety of fabrics available to you and see how an experienced shop owner has combined fabrics.

One simple approach to combining fabrics for a quilt is to choose one fabric that contains several colors and then select coordinating fabrics in colors used in the theme fabric.

Fabric color is not the only factor to consider when combining fabrics. To increase the visual texture of your quilts, choose fabrics with small, medium, and large scale printed designs. As you combine printed fabrics, choose ones that have the same mood or degree of sophistication. Fabric printed with baby rattles and baby bottles will probably not work well with sophisticated tropical prints or in a quilt for your husband or teenage son.

In order for the design to "read" in your quilt, you will need contrast in value—light, medium, and dark—so that some design elements advance or are predominant and others recede and create the background.

Purchasing Fabric

The materials list with each of the projects in this book gives the amount of each fabric needed. We always allow for some extra fabric in our estimates, as much as ½ yard for the major fabrics in the quilt and ⅛ to ¼ yard for other fabrics.

In our materials lists, and possibly in other quilt publications, you will notice the terms "fat quarter" and "fat eighth." These terms describe special ways cotton fabric can be cut into quarter-yard and eighth-yard pieces. Quilters like these cuts because the pieces are easier to work with and also allow for cutting larger pieces then conventional cuts do.

A normal quarter yard cut would be 9" deep by approximately 42" wide (the width of the fabric from selvage to selvage). A "fat quarter" is the same amount of fabric, but cut differently. The store clerk cuts a half yard (18" deep by 42" wide), and then cuts it in half at the fabric fold— resulting in a piece that is 18" x 21". This

MARIANNE SAYS: Sometimes we choose a theme fabric and end up not purchasing it— we just use it to inspire a great color combination.

"chunk" of fabric is much easier to wash, press, and cut than the alternative long, skinny, normal quarter yard.

The normal eighth yard is only 4½" deep by approximately 42" long. If you throw half a dozen of these in the washing machine, the result is almost as bad as six pairs of panty hose laundered together! The much-preferred "fat eighth" is created when the store clerk cuts a normal quarter yard (9" x 42") and then cuts it in half at the fold—resulting in a piece of fabric 9" x 21".

When you visit a quilt shop, you will probably see baskets and bins of fat quarters and fat eighths already cut and priced to sell. Quilters buy them not only because these special cuts are so much easier to use, but also to avoid having to wait for the fabric to be cut.

Preparing Fabric

We recommend that you wash, dry, and press fabrics before using them in quilts. Washing preshrinks the fabric, and removes excess sizing, chemical finishes, and dye. You can throw like colors in with the family laundry. We prewash fabrics in warm water and detergent or Orvus Paste soap (available at quilt shops or livestock supply stores), dry them at a medium or permanent-press setting in the dryer, and steam iron as needed to remove wrinkles.

Some dark fabrics bleed or release dye during washing. To test a fabric for color fastness, stop your washer during the final rinse. Scoop out some rinse water in a clear glass and look for color. If the fabric is still bleeding, wash it again. If it continues to release color, don't use it in your quilt, or use it only with fabrics of similar color.

Storing Fabric

We like to store small patchwork pieces, miscellaneous fabric scraps, and assorted sewing notions in sandwich-size, quart-size, and gallon-size plastic bags with zipper-type closures. Use a permanent marker to label bags. Large pizza boxes are just right for storing and carrying around completed blocks. (Ask for clean boxes at a local pizzeria.) Line the bottom of the box with a square of low-loft batting to keep the blocks from sliding around. Plastic sweater boxes are perfect containers to store folded fabric pieces and fabric strips.

FABRIC CUTTING BASICS

Rotary cutting generally begins with cutting strips, and then cutting those strips into smaller pieces or combining them with other strips to make strip sets.

Cut all strips across the fabric <u>width,</u> that is, <u>selvage to selvage.</u> On page 9, we show you how to fold your fabric in fourths to make cutting easier. Our instructions for projects tell you how wide to cut strips, how many strips to cut from each fabric, and the number and size of pieces to sub-cut from each strip. The cutting dimensions we give you for strips and pieces include ¼" seam allowances.

CUTTING STRIPS AND BASIC PIECES
Squaring up Fabric and Cutting Strips

Before you cut strips or other pieces from fabric, straighten or square-off one end by trimming it so that the cut edge is at a right angle to the selvages.

1. Begin by folding fabric in half lengthwise, matching selvage edges. Hold the fabric up off the table and slide the matched selvage edges in opposite directions until the fabric hangs straight. If the fabric hangs with a crease or buckle in it as shown in Photo #1, it's not straight. Keep adjusting the selvages until the fabric hangs smooth as shown in Photo #2.

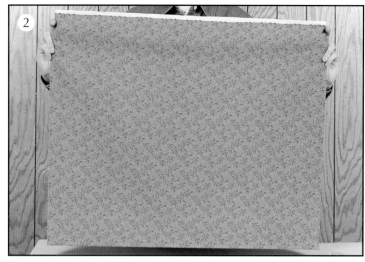

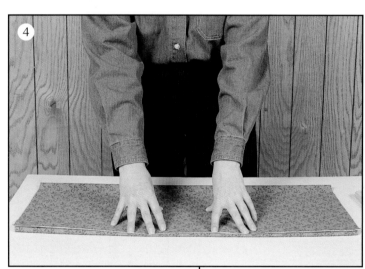

2. Lay the folded fabric on a cutting mat with selvages nearest you; fold the fabric in half lengthwise again (Photo #3), bringing selvages to center fold (Photo #4). By folding fabric in fourths, cuts will be a manageable 11" wide.

LIZ SAYS:
You may need to misalign cut edges to get selvages to line up and fabric to hang straight; pressing out the center fold can make this easier.

MARIANNE SAYS:
If you are right-handed, you will square off and begin cutting strips from the left edge of the fabric. If you are left-handed, you will square off and begin cutting strips from the right edge of the fabric.

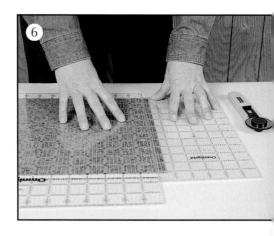

LIZ SAYS:
Check frequently to see that cuts remain perpendicular to the fold. If strips are not cut at a true right angle to folded fabric, they will bow (Photo #11). If necessary, refold fabric and square it off again to produce straight strips.

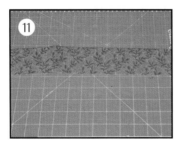

3. Place a large ruled square on the fabric, aligning a horizontal line with the folded edge of the fabric and positioning the left edge approximately ½" from the uneven fabric end (Photo #5). Position your 6" x 12" ruler against the left edge of the square (Photo #6). Remove the square but keep the ruler in place.
4. Holding ruler firmly in place, cut along edge of ruler (Photo #7), trimming uneven fabric edge from end of fabric (Photo #8). Exert firm and even pressure on the cutter as you roll it away from yourself.
5. Position the ruler atop the folded fabric a the squared-off edge so that it measures the desired strip width. Cut through all layers, guiding cutter along edge of ruler (Photo #9 to cut a perfectly straight strip (Photo #10).

Cutting Squares, Rectangles, and Triangles from Strips

Depending on how many squares or rectangles you need for the pattern you are making, you can either unfold your cut strip or leave it folded in fourths (or in half) and cut it into the shapes you need. For the blocks in this book, you will mostly be cutting squares and rectangles since we use the "diagonal seams" method to make triangle units from simple squares and rectangles. For a few blocks, you will need to cut squares into triangles.

Squares and Rectangles

1. Using your 6" x 12" ruler and your large folded square, square-off the end of the strip and remove the selvage edges in the same way you squared off the uneven fabric end.
2. Align the desired measurements on the 6" x 12" ruler with the straight strip end and cut across the strip, cutting the desired number of squares or rectangles (Photo #1).
3. To cut pieces longer than the 6" width of your ruler, either position the ruler lengthwise to measure and cut (Photo #2), or use your large square to measure and cut (Photo #3).

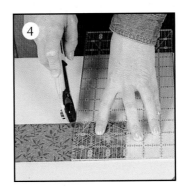

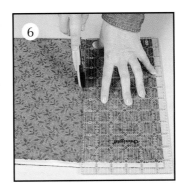

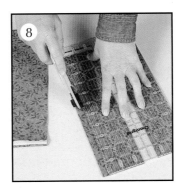

MARIANNE SAYS:
Here's another way to cut squares and rectangles from a folded strip--and square off the ends at the same time. Cut a wider segment than needed from the strip (Photo #4), then rotate it around and cut the needed units. (Photo #5). By making the wider cut, you use enough of your ruler to be sure you are cutting at a perfect right angle to the strip edges. You can also use this method for cutting strips from your folded yardage. For example, if you need lots of 2½" strips, first make a 5½" cut that includes the uneven edges (Photo #6). Then, rotate the cut segment so that you can align the 2½" measurement along the clean cut (Photo #7). Cut one strip, then another. What you have left is the uneven waste (Photo #8).

Triangles

You'll need two types of triangles to make the blocks in this book. Although other kinds of triangles are sometimes used in patchwork blocks, these two basic triangle types are the most common in all patchwork. Both are right-angle triangles. We refer to the first type as "half-square triangles" and the other type as "quarter-square triangles."

Half-Square Triangles

Half-square triangles are right-angle triangles created by cutting a square in half diagonally to make two triangles. The two legs (short sides) are on the straight of grain of the fabric, and the hypotenuse (long side) is on the bias. Pairs of contrasting half-square triangles are often joined along the long sides of the triangles to form half-square triangle units.

Cutting Half-Square Triangles

1. Add ⅞" to the desired finished measurement of the triangle legs. Cut a beginning square this size as shown in Photo #1. For example, for a half-square triangle with 2" finished legs, cut a 2⅞" square.
2. Cut the beginning square in half diagonally from corner to corner to make 2 half-square triangles as shown in Photo #2.

Making Half-Square Triangle Units

1. Join pairs of triangles together along the long diagonal edges as shown in Photo #3. Be careful not to pull or stretch the bias edges as you sew.

2. Position the unit on your ironing board with the darker triangle facing up. Set the seam with your iron (Photo #4).

MARIANNE SAYS:
The extra ⅞" added to the beginning square will automatically add ¼" seam allowances to all three sides of the half-square triangles.

LIZ SAYS:
If you need lots of half-square triangles, begin by cutting several strips of fabric the needed width. Cut squares from the strips. Cut the squares in half diagonally into half-square triangles.

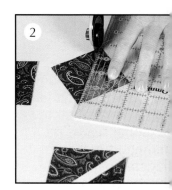

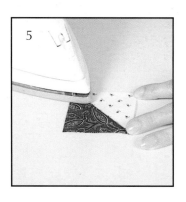

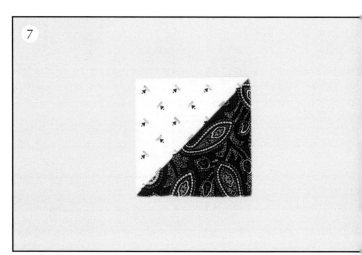

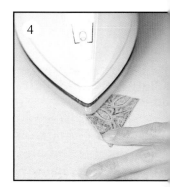

. Open out the darker triangle and use the tip of the iron to open the seam (Photo #5). Make sure there are no pleats along the seam.

. Trim the small points of seam allowances that extend beyond the edges (Photo #6) to complete the unit (Photo #7).

Quarter-Square Triangles

Quarter-square triangles are right-angle triangles created by cutting a square diagonally in both directions to make four triangles.

The hypotenuse (long side) of the triangle is on the straight of the fabric grain, and the two legs (short sides) are on the bias.

Quarter-square triangles are needed for blocks like Wheels (page 38) where the hypotenuse (long side) of the triangles falls to the outside of the block or block units. Keeping the outside edges of a block on the fabric straight of grain is a good patchwork rule-of-thumb. If the outsides are on the bias, the edges stretch, and the blocks don't remain square.

Cutting Quarter-Square Triangles

1. Add 1¼" to the desired finished measurement of the hypotenuse (long side) of the triangle. Cut a beginning square this size. For example, for a quarter-square triangle with a 5" finished hypotenuse, cut a 6¼" beginning square.

2. Cut the beginning square diagonally in both directions (in an "X") to make 4 quarter-square triangles as shown in Photo #1.

MARIANNE SAYS:
The extra 1¼" added to the beginning square will automatically add ¼" seam allowances to all three sides of the quarter-square triangles.

LIZ SAYS:
If you need lots of quarter-square triangles, begin by cutting a strip of fabric the width of your beginning square. Cut squares from the strip. Cut the squares diagonally in both directions to make quarter-square triangles.

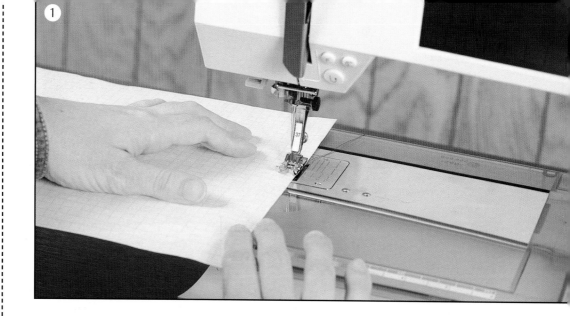

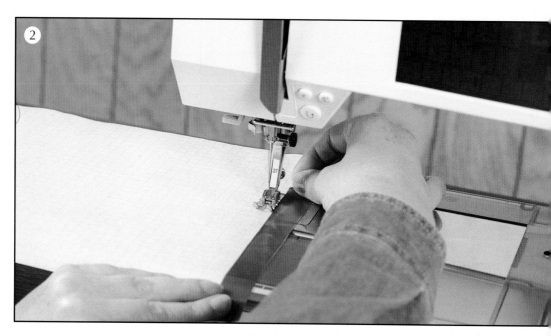

MACHINE PATCHWORK BASICS

The standard width for patchwork seams is ¼". If your seam is not ¼" wide, your patchwork pieces will not fit together, the corners and points on your patchwork pieces will not match, and your projects will turn out the wrong size.

The Patchwork Seam

On some machines, the distance from the needle to the edge of the standard presser foot is exactly ¼". If your presser foot is not ¼", you can order a "patchwork foot" from your dealer or a sewing machine repair shop. On some machines, another option is to move the needle position to gauge an exact ¼" seam. On some machines the throat plate may be marked with a ¼" sewing guide or you can add a masking tape seam guide to your throat plate as described below. Once you make the seam guide, <u>sew the test seam.</u> <u>If your patchwor fails the test, adjust the guide!</u>

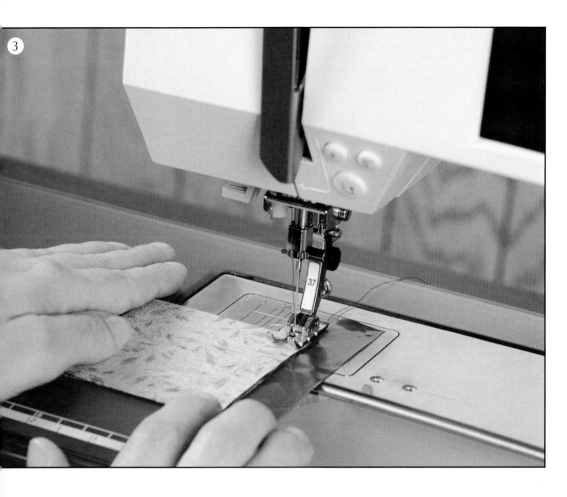

(3)

Making a Seam Guide
1. Use your rotary cutting ruler to mark a thin line ¼" from the edge of a piece of paper, or use ¼" ruled graph paper.
2. Put the paper under the presser foot and lower the needle through the line. Lower the foot and adjust the paper so it is parallel with the edge of the foot (Photo #1).
3. Lay a strip of masking tape along the paper's edge (Photo #2).

4. Sew a test seam as described below using your new masking tape seam guide and adjust as needed to achieve the proper seam width.

Sewing a Test Seam
1. Cut two 3" squares of fabric.
2. Set your machine to stitch 12-15 stitches per inch, usually a 2.5 setting on imported machines.

3. Align cut edges of squares and sew them together along one side, using ¼" presser foot or tape edge as a guide (Photo #3). Press seam allowances to one side.
4. Measure across the squares. The seamed squares should measure 5½". If your measurement is not 5½", adjust your seam width and re-test.

LIZ SAYS:
I cannot stress enough the importance of sewing a test seam and measuring the test patchwork! Adjust your presser foot or masking tape guide for as long as it takes to achieve the 5½" patchwork measurement.

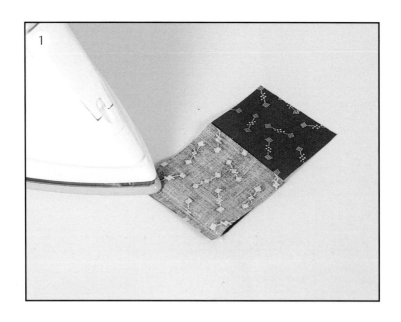

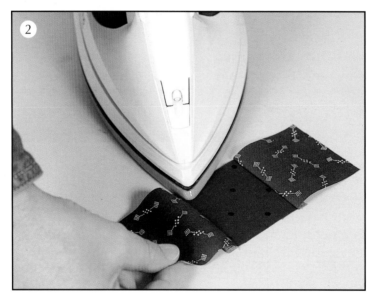

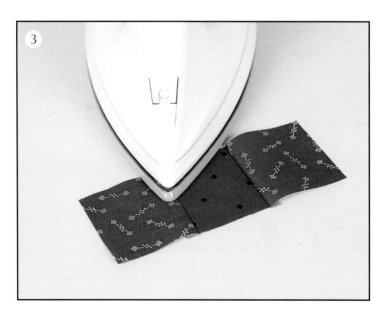

PRESSING POINTERS

Quilters have strong opinions about pressing patchwork. Some advocate steam, while others say a dry iron is best. Some like to press from the wrong side of a block, and some like to press from the top. We like steam, if it's used right, and we have definite ideas about how seams should be pressed. We've tried lots of ways over our years of sewing, and this is our favorite method.

Press, Don't Iron

Always *press,* rather than *iron,* your patchwork pieces. The goal in *ironing,* or sliding the iron from place to place on the fabric, is to remove wrinkles. Sliding the iron can stretch the fabrics and distort fabric pieces. Remember when you press your patchwork pieces: They aren't wrinkled!

To *press,* each time you move the iron to a new position, pick it up and set it back down gently. Your goals in pressing are to open the seam fully without creating any pleats and to set the seam allowances to one side.

Pressing Procedure

1. With pieces right sides facing as you stitched them, set the seam by bringing the iron down on the seam. This embeds the threads and smoothes and evens out the stitching (Photo #1).

2. Open out the top piece of fabric, the one you want to press the seam allowance toward. Use the tip of the iron to open the seam. As you work, make sure to press the seam fully open with no pleats or tucks along the seam (Photo #2).

3. When you are sure there are no pleats along the seam, set the opened seam with the iron (Photo #3).

4. Plan your pressing strategy so that seams are pressed in opposite directions where corners of patchwork pieces will meet. This makes matching corners and points easier and reduces bulk at these locations (Photo #4).

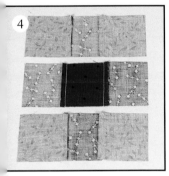

SOME
PRESSING
RULES-OF-THUMB

1. Set seams by pressing them with right sides together. Then press seam allowances to one side.

2. Press toward dark fabrics when possible. If you press a dark fabric toward a light one, the darker seam allowance might show through the top of the quilt. Keep in mind, however, that your goal is for seams to lie smooth and flat, and that as long as the fabrics in your quilt are not extremely light or extremely dark, you don't need to worry about seam allowances showing through.

3. Always press a seam before crossing it with another seam or joining seamed pieces.

4. Press seam allowances to one side rather than open. Seams pressed in one direction are much stronger than seams pressed open. Batting fibers can escape through open seams. Seams pressed to one side can often be abutted with other seams when joining patchwork units, resulting in nice, crisp corners and tidy, flat blocks.

5. Remember that pressing is not the same as ironing. Your patchwork is not wrinkled! Position your iron gently on your work. Don't slide it around or you may stretch fabrics and distort pieces.

PATCHWORK BLOCK LESSONS

Your first patchwork quilt begins with your first patchwork blocks. The following nine lessons will take you step-by-step through making the nine blocks you need for the Seams Sew Fun sampler pictured. We're showing it in two versions, one with blocks oriented vertically and one with blocks oriented horizontally. The same nine blocks are used in each quilt. The project measures 29" x 37", a good size for a wall quilt or crib quilt.

All you need to get started are the tools and supplies described in "Getting Started Basics" on pages 6 - 7, and the fabric amounts listed below. Take the fabric shopping list to your local quilt shop or fabric store, or call Fons & Porter Quilt Supply at 888-985-1020 to order a kit.

Materials for Sampler Quilt

1 yard of dark fabric for outer borders, binding, and patchwork blocks

½ yard of 2nd dark fabric for narrow inner border and patchwork blocks

Fat quarter (18" x 22") each of:
- 4 background fabrics (cream) OR 1 yard of 1 background fabric
- 7 medium/dark fabrics (at least 1 green)

Cutting for Borders

From the 1 yard of dark fabric, cut and set aside:
- 4 (3½"-wide) strips for outer borders.
- 4 (2¼"-wide) strips for binding.

From the ½ yard of 2nd dark fabric, cut and set aside:
- 4 (1"-wide) strips for narrow inner border.

QUILTER'S TIP–SETTING UP YOUR MACHINE FOR THE DIAGONAL SEAMS METHOD

We use the popular "diagonal seams" stitching technique for many patchwork units because it enables us to easily create types of patchwork units that would ordinarily involve complicated cutting. Many kinds of triangle units, for example, can be made just by cutting and sewing combinations of squares and rectangles—without ever cutting a triangle! This method usually involves placing a square atop some other shape and sewing from one corner to the opposite diagonal corner of the square—thus the name, "diagonal seams."

Key to successful diagonal seams sewing is stitching a perfectly straight seam from corner to corner. Some quilters, concerned that their stitching won't be straight, have resorted to actually drawing the sewing line with pencil, or folding the top square in half diagonally and creasing it to form a stitching guideline. We don't advocate these methods because they take time. Instead, we like to set up our machines in a special way that ensures straight stitching. Here's how to set up your machine.

1. Raise the presser foot and lower the needle to a fully "down" position. Place a ruler atop the throat plate of your machine, gently resting the edge of the ruler against the needle as shown in Photo A. Lower the presser foot, making sure the edge of the ruler is exactly parallel to the needle.

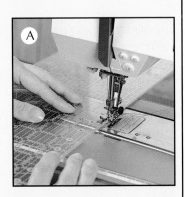

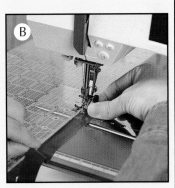

2. Place a piece of masking or other type of tape on the flatbed of the machine, right along the edge of the ruler as shown in Photo B. Lift the presser foot and remove the ruler. Raise the machine needle. The tape is in a straight line from your machine needle to the front edge of your machine. You will use the tape guide when feeding diagonal-seams units through your machine. The guide will keep your stitching straight. You will use this technique in Lesson #1.

LIZ SAYS:
Incorporate the remaining portions of these border fabrics into some of your patchwork blocks to give your project cohesiveness.

LESSON #1
FARMER'S DAUGHTER BLOCK
(10" finished)

Farmer's Daughter is a good block to start with. You'll make a traditional nine patch unit for the center and learn to use the diagonal seams piecing method to sew patchwork pieces for the sides.

Cutting

As you cut your pieces, lay them out like Photo #1.

From background fabric, cut:
- 4 (2½") A squares
- 4 (2½" x 6½") rectangles for C

From 1st dark fabric, cut:
- 8 (2½") squares for B triangles

From 2nd and 3rd dark fabrics, cut:
- 9 (2½") A squares for center nine patch (You will probably want to cut 5 squares from one color and 4 squares from a second color OR 4 squares from each fabric and a center square from your 1st dark fabric.)

LIZ SAYS:
A "Nine Patch" is a simple block made of nine squares-- three rows of three squares per row. Quilters refer to many blocks that divide up into three even rows of units as having "nine patch construction."

MARIANNE SAYS:
Seam allowances are pressed in opposite directions where corners of squares meet. This is called abutting seams. This pressing method enables you to match corners and reduces bulk where seams meet.

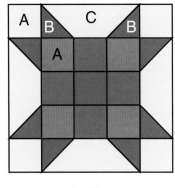
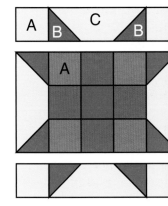

Block Diagram

Piecing Diagram

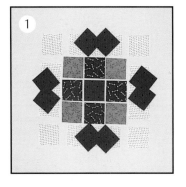
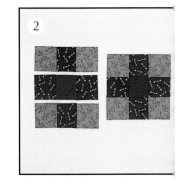

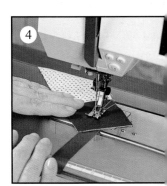

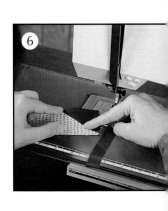

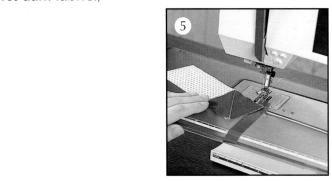

ake the Center
ine Patch

Using a ¼" seam, in the nine squares r the center nine atch in 3 rows of squares per row.

Press seams toward arker fabrics. See ressing Pointers on age 16 for perfect ressing habits.

Join rows to omplete nine patch nit as shown in hoto #2.

lake the Side Units

With right sides cing, place a B square top one end of a rectangle. Place the nit under the sewing machine presser foot s shown in Photo #3. ee Setting Up Your Machine for the Diagonal Seams Method on page 19.

Using the tape as a uide, stitch diagonally cross B square as hown in Photo #4. eep the lower corner f the square aligned vith the left edge of our tape to guide you cross the diagonal.

Remove the unit rom the sewing machine (Photo #5).

Open out triangle ormed by your titching and "finger ress" seam open vith your fingernail Photo #6). Make sure hat corners of bottom nd top fabric line up venly. If they don't, ou haven't sewn a erfect diagonal from corner to corner and ou'll need to take out he seam and sew it gain.

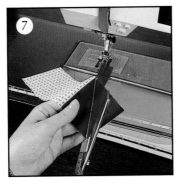

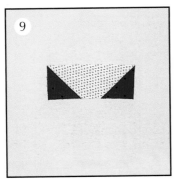

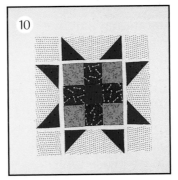

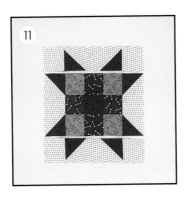

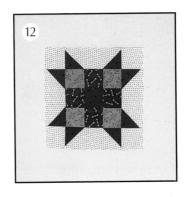

5. Flip triangle back, and use scissors to trim excess fabric, cutting approximately ¼" away from stitching (Photo #7). You will be cutting two layers of fabric.

6. Place a second B square atop the opposite end of the C rectangle. Stitch as shown in Photo #8.

7. Finger press and trim as before to complete 1 B/C unit (Photo #9). Make 4 B/C units.

Assemble the Block

1. Lay out the center nine patch, the 4 B/C units, and 4 A squares (Photo #10).

2. Join A squares to opposite ends of 2 B/C units. Press seam allowances toward squares.

3. Join B/C units to 2 opposite sides of nine patch (Photo #11). Press seam allowances toward nine patch.

4. Join the 3 rows, abutting seams. Set seams and press to complete block (Photo #12).

MARIANNE SAYS:
Liz and I have been sewing patchwork for years, but we still make mistakes. The best way to take out a seam is to use your seam ripper and cut every third or fourth thread on one side. Turn the piece over and simply pull on one end of the thread on the opposite side. It will pull out just like pulling the string on a sack of pet food!

LIZ SAYS:
The Nine Patch is one of quilting's most basic blocks. In the nineteenth century, little girls were taught to sew patchwork at about age 4, usually by making a nine patch quilt for their dolls. If you like the Nine Patch, you might like to make our pretty blue and white Nine Patch Crib Quilt. Instructions are on pages 42 - 45.

LESSON #2
TREE BLOCK
(4" x 8" finished)

Our tree design is made of stacked patchwork units we call goose chase units. Goose Chase is a traditional patchwork pattern. Goose chase units are sometimes combined in long strips to make a quilt, but they also appear as parts of many patchwork blocks. You will make goose chase units for this block, the Star Block, and the Jack-in-the-Box Block to include in your sampler. All goose chase units are made with 2 squares and 1 rectangle (Photo #1).

Cutting

From background fabric, cut:
- 6 (2½") squares for A triangles
- 2 (2½" x 2") C rectangles

From green fabric, cut:
- 3 (2½" x 4½") rectangles for B triangles. These can be all one fabric or three different fabrics.

From brown fabric, cut:
- 1 (2½" x 1½") D rectangle

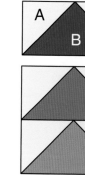

Block Diagram

Piecing Diagram

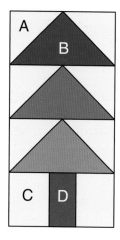
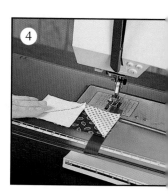

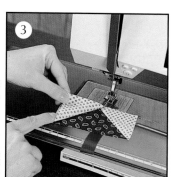
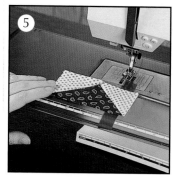
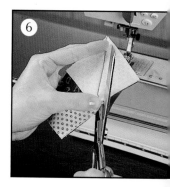

Make the Goose Chase Units

1. With right sides facing, place an A square atop one end of a B rectangle. Use your tape guideline and stitch diagonally as shown in Photo #2.

2. Open out triangle formed and finger press seam open. Check that corners are aligned squarely. Flip triangle back and trim off excess fabric, leaving approximately ¼" for seam allowance.

3. Place a second A square right sides together atop the opposite end of the B piece. Gently fold the square back on the diagonal to check the angle you will stitch (Photo #3).

4. Stitch diagonally, using your tape guide. Remove the unit from the sewing machine (Photo #4).

5. Open out second triangle, finger press seam, and trim excess fabric (Photos #5 and #6).

6. Make a total of three goose chase units.

Assemble the Block

1. Join three goose chase units to make tree top (Photo #7). See Sewing through the "X", this page.

2. Lay out the two light fabric C rectangles and the brown D rectangle as shown in Photo #8.

3. Join the strips. Press seam allowances toward the trunk.

4. Join trunk to bottom of tree top to complete the block (Photo #9).

QUILTER'S TIP–SEWING THROUGH THE "X"

When joining goose chase units to each other, or incorporating them in other blocks, stitch whenever possible with the goose chase unit on top so you can "stitch through the X," as shown in Photo A.

Stitching through the X ensures neat, "pointy" points for your goose chase triangles (Photo B).

Blunted points (Photo C) occur when the seam is too wide and misses the "X"(Photo D).

Floating points, those that don't meet the adjoining unit (Photo E), occur when the seam is too narrow (Photo F).

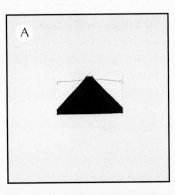
A

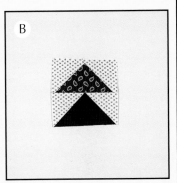
B

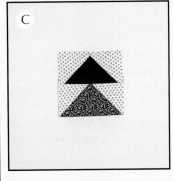
C

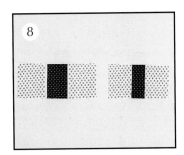
D

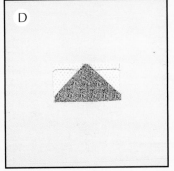
E

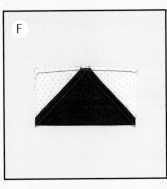
F

7

8

9

LIZ SAYS:
Although not correct, floating points are usually less noticeable than blunted ones.

STAR BLOCK
(4" finished)

This basic star appears in many patchwork quilts. It goes by names such as Eight Pointed Star, Sawtooth Star, or Simple Star. The Star Block for your sampler quilt is a small one, just 4" finished. As a bonus, we've included a cutting chart on page 25 for stars ranging from 4" to 12" (finished) so you can try this popular block in other sizes.

For this block, you'll use a piecing diagram, rather than step-by-step photos, to make the goose chase units for the block. Quilting books generally provide diagrams like this to guide you through block construction. Knowing how to read such diagrams is a valuable skill for any patchworker.

Cutting

From background fabric, cut:
- 4 (1½") C squares
- 4 (1½" x 2½") rectangles for B triangles

From 1st dark fabric, cut:
- 8 (1½") squares for A triangles (star points)

From 2nd dark fabric, cut:
- 1 (2½") D square (star center)

LIZ SAYS:
If you need to review making goose chase units, see page 23.

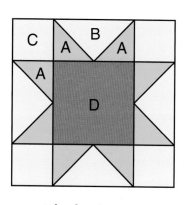

Block Diagram

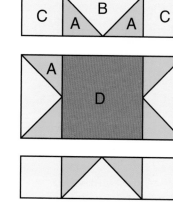

Piecing Diagram

Goose Chase Unit Diagonal Seams Diagrams

Make the Goose Chase Units

1. With right sides facing, place an A square atop one end of a B rectangle as shown in Piecing Diagram. Use your tape guideline and stitch diagonally from corner to corner. Finger press, and trim excess fabric.

2. Place a second A square atop the opposite end of the B piece. Stitch, press, and trim.

3. Repeat to make 4 goose chase units.

Assemble the Block

1. Lay out the D center square, 4 goose chase units, and 4 C squares as shown in diagram.

2. Join C squares to opposite ends of 2 goose chase units (Photo #1). Press seam allowances toward squares. Join goose chase units to 2 opposite sides of D square. Press seam allowances toward square.

3. Join rows to complete block (Photo #2).

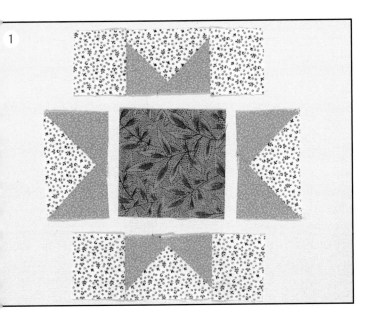

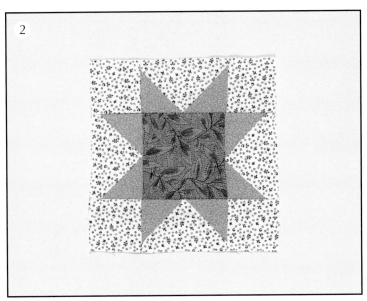

STAR BLOCK CUTTING CHART

To make Star Blocks in other sizes, use the bonus cutting chart below. Simply choose a finished block size in the left-hand column, then read across for the size of the pieces you must cut from each fabric to achieve your finished block size. Follow the instructions for the 4" block to complete your larger Star Blocks.

Finished Block Size	From background fabric, cut 4 C squares	From background fabric, cut 4 rectangles for B triangles	From 1st dark fabric, cut 8 squares for A triangles	From 2nd dark fabric, cut 1 D square
4"	1½"	1½" x 2½"	1½"	2½"
5"	1¾"	1¾" x 3"	1¾"	3"
6"	2"	2" x 3½"	2"	3½"
7"	2¼"	2¼" x 4"	2¼"	4"
8"	2½"	2½" x 4½"	2½"	4½"
9"	2¾"	2¾" x 5"	2¾"	5"
10"	3"	3" x 5½"	3"	5½"
11"	3¼"	3¼" x 6"	3¼"	6"
12"	3½"	3½" x 6½"	3½"	6½"

The diagonal seams method involves trimming off and discarding two small triangles each time you stitch a unit. Generally, the discard triangles are small, and the minimal amount of waste is a trade off for easy cutting and piecing.

For bigger units, however, the waste triangles are larger and harder to throw away. Here's a method you can use to keep from wasting any fabric. It involves making a second line of stitching parallel to the first. See Ideas for Using Half-Square Triangle Units, page 27.

Set Up for Double Sewing

1. Raise your sewing machine presser foot and place a ruler on the throat plate, positioning the ruler so that 1/2" extends beyond the left edge of the tape guide you made for sewing diagonal seams. Lower the presser foot to hold the ruler in place.

2. Make a second tape guide 1/2" away from the first one by positioning a strip of tape along the extended edge of the ruler (Photo A). Remove the ruler.

Double Sewing

1. After stitching two pieces of fabric together for a diagonal seam unit, remove the patchwork from the machine and sew again, this time guiding the lower corner of the top fabric through the machine along the edge

of the second tape guide (Photo B).

2. When sewing is complete, remove the work from the machine and cut between the two lines of stitching (Photo C). You will have your diagonal seams unit plus a bonus half-square triangle (Photos D and E).

3. To complete bonus half-square triangle, press seam and then trim unit to square it up

and make it a usable size. To trim, place 6" ruled square atop half-square triangle, aligning 45° line with seam. Trim 2 adjacent sides. Determine size you want to cut half-square triangle. Place 6" ruled square atop half-square triangle so that measurements on ruler are aligned with sides you just trimmed. Then trim 2 remaining adjacent sides.

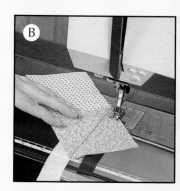

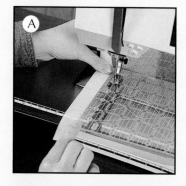

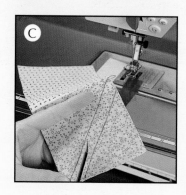

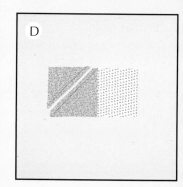

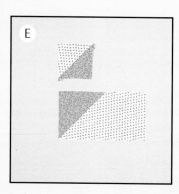

MARIANNE SAYS: A 6" ruled square that has a 45° diagonal line is a helpful tool for trimming bonus half-square triangles accurately.

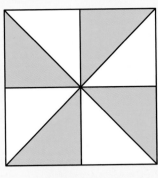
Pinwheel Block

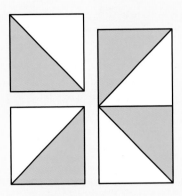
Piecing Diagram

Instructions
1. Trim half-square triangle units to desired finished size plus ½" for seam allowances. This block is 2 x 2 units, so block will finish twice as large as each finished unit. For example, for a 4" finished block, begin with 2½" trimmed bonus half-square triangle units.

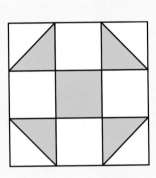
Shoo Fly Block

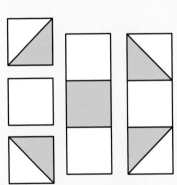
Piecing Diagram

Instructions
1. Trim half-square triangle units to desired finished size plus ½" for seam allowances. This block is 3 x 3 units, so block will finish 3 times the size of each finished unit. For example, for a 6" finished block, begin with 2½" trimmed bonus half-square triangle units.
2. Cut 1 dark and 4 light squares the same size as your half-square triangle units (2½").
3. Join units in rows. Join rows to complete block.

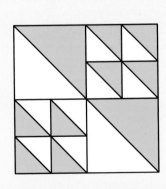
Flock of Geese Block

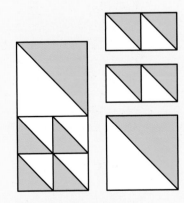
Piecing Diagram

Instructions
1. You will need two sizes of half square triangle units. The small units are half the finished size of the larger units. Cut units to include an extra ½" for seam allowances. For example, cut 2½" small units and 4½" large units for an 8" finished block.
2. Join sets of 4 small half-square triangle units into a square. Arrange these units and larger half-square triangle units and join as shown in the Piecing Diagram.

HOUSE BLOCK

(8" x 12" finished)

The House Block is a "representational" or "realistic" block because it resembles a real house. Other representational blocks in your sampler are the Star and Sailboat Blocks. When you build your House Block, you'll use the diagonal seams method to make piecing the chimney section and creating the roof section easy. If you like this block, think about making the Hearth and Home Wall Quilt on page 46.

Cutting

From background fabric, cut:
- 1 (4½") square for A
- 1 (2½" x 4½") rectangle for B
- 1 (1½" x 4½") rectangle for D

From house fabric, cut:
- 1 (2½" x 8½") F rectangle
- 1 (2½" x 3½") G rectangle
- 1 (2½" x 6½") K rectangle
- 2 (1½" x 6½") I rectangles

From chimney fabric, cut:
- 1 (1½" x 4½") rectangle for C

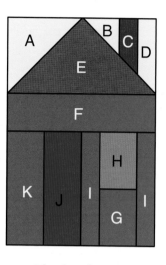

Block Diagram

From roof fabric, cut:
- 1 (4½" x 8½") rectangle for E

From door fabric, cut:
- 1 (2½" x 6½") J rectangle

From window fabric, cut:
- 1 (2½" x 3½") H rectangle

Make the Roof Unit

1. Lay out background pieces B and D and chimney C and join as shown in Photo #1.
2. With right sides facing, lay B/C/D unit from Step 1 atop roof piece E. Place Step 1 unit so that chimney is parallel to bottom edge of roof piece. Gently fold back chimney unit to make sure chimney will be pointed up

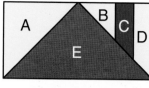

Piecing Diagram

when seam is sewn (Photo #2). (If you position the unit with the chimney positioned vertically, you'll have an "oops" chimney like the one in Photo #3!)
3. Stitch diagonally as shown in Photo #4, press, and trim.
4. Lay background square A atop opposite end of roof piece. Gently fold back corner to check the correct angle to sew diagonal seam (Photo #5).
5. Stitch diagonally to complete roof unit (Photo #6). Press and trim.

Make House Section

1. Lay out house pieces G, I and K, window H, and door J as shown in Photo #7.
2. Join house piece G and window H. Sew the I piece to right-hand side of G/H unit as shown in piecing diagram. Press seam allowances toward piece.
3. Join door J and house piece K. Add remaining piece to right-hand side of J/K unit.
4. Join the units as shown in the photo to complete the house section.

Assemble the Block

1. Lay out roof unit, house piece F, and house section as shown in Photo #8.
2. Join pieces to complete House Block (Photo #9).

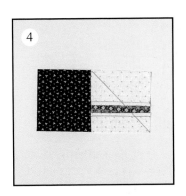

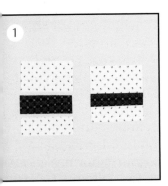

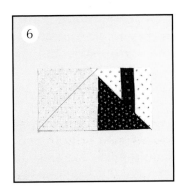

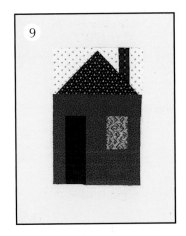

JACK-IN-THE BOX BLOCK
(10" finished)

The Jack-in-the-Box Block has a center bar dividing four identical quadrants that rotate pinwheel fashion (either clockwise or counter-clockwise—you can choose) around the block. This block calls for four goose chase units, plus four units we call "goofy geese." Goofy geese are similar to regular goose chase units, except that, for goofy geese units, the two lines of diagonal stitching run parallel to each other, instead of at two different angles. If you have ever "goofed up" a regular goose chase unit, you've already made one of these units.

Cutting
From background fabric, cut:
• 16 (2½") squares for A

From 1st dark fabric, cut:
• 8 (2½" x 4½") rectangles for B and C

From 2nd dark fabric, cut:
• 4 (2½" x 4½") D rectangles

From 3rd dark fabric, cut:
• 1 (2½") E square

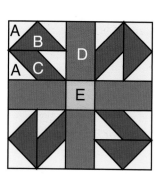

Block Diagram

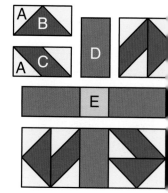

Piecing Diagram

Goose Chase Unit Diagonal Seams Diagrams

Make "Goofy Geese"
1. Lay 1 A square atop 1 C rectangle. Stitch diagonally, press, and trim (Photo #1).
2. Lay 1 A square atop opposite end of C rectangle. Gently fold back corner of square to check angle to sew (Photo #2). For this unit, the two seams must run parallel to one another.
3. Stitch diagonally. Remove unit from sewing machine (Photo #3). Open square to check stitching angle and corner alignment (Photo #4). Finger press and trim excess triangles.
4. Repeat to make 4 identical units.

Assemble the Block
1. Using 2 A squares and 1 B rectangle, construct 1 goose chase unit. Refer to Goose Chase Piecing Diagrams, above.
2. Repeat to make a total of 4 units.
3. Join 1 normal goose chase unit and 1 goofy goose unit as shown in Piecing Diagram. Repeat to make 4 identical quadrants.
4. Lay out quadrants, 4 D rectangles, and 1 E square in 3 rows as shown.
5. Join units to form rows. Press seam allowances toward D rectangles.
6. Join rows to complete block (Photo #5).

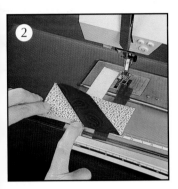

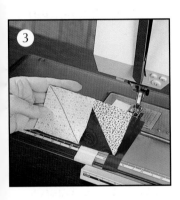

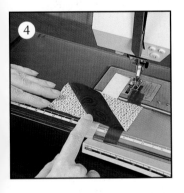

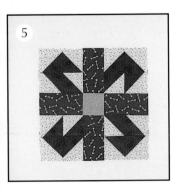

QUILTER'S TIP–ASSEMBLY LINE PIECING AND PRESSING

The more comfortable you become with patchwork, the more interested you will be in speeding up each step. (Speedier methods mean you can start the next quilt sooner!) We use "chain piecing" and "assembly line" pressing whenever possible.

Chain Piecing

Chain piecing is feeding units into your sewing machine one after another without cutting the thread (Photo A) until a whole group is completed.

Chain piecing prevents small pieces from being dragged down into the machine throat plate at the beginning of seams. It saves time because you repeat the same process without stopping to clip threads. And, it saves thread!

One disadvantage of chaining is that if you make a mistake, you make multiples of it instead of just a single boo-boo. Also, when you're deep into a chain piecing session, check your pieces frequently to make sure you have bobbin thread. We have often "air stitched" dozens of units before discovering they weren't getting joined!

Assembly Line Pressing

Assembly line pressing goes hand-in-hand with chain piecing. For efficient pressing, press like units in groups and keep them organized in stacks (Photo B).

WEATHERVANE BLOCK
(12" finished)

You'll use the diagonal seams method to make the four side units for the Weathervane Block. We call these "long goose" units because they are similar to regular goose chase units but have a square instead of a rectangle as a base. You'll also join half-square triangles to make half-square triangle units, one of the most common elements in all patchwork.

Cutting
From background, cut:
- 12 (2½") squares (4 A squares and 8 for C)
- 4 (2⅞") squares for B. Cut each square in half diagonally to make 8 B half-square triangles. (See Half-Square Triangles, page 12.)

From 1st dark fabric, cut:
- 4 (2½") A squares
- 1 (4½") E square
- 4 (2⅞") squares for B. Cut each square in half diagonally to make 8 B half-square triangles. (See Half-Square Triangles, page 12.)

From 2nd dark fabric, cut:
- 4 (4½") squares for D

LIZ SAYS:
These pieces are similar to goose chase units but you sew small squares to a large square rather than a rectangle.

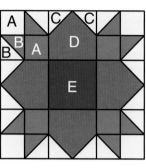
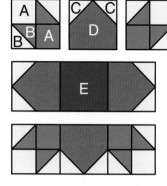

Block Diagram   **Piecing Diagram**

Goose Chase Unit Diagonal Seams Diagrams

Make the Long Goose Units
1. Place 1 (2½") C square atop 1 corner of 1 (4½") D square. Stitch diagonally, press, and open seam (Photo #1).
2. Place a second C square atop the opposite side of D square. Stitch, press and trim to complete "long goose" side unit (Photo #2).

Make the Corner Units
1. Join pairs of background fabric B triangles and dark fabric B triangles to make 8 half-square triangle units. See Half-Square Triangles, page 12.
2. Join half-square triangles with 2½" light A squares and 2½" dark A squares to form 8 partial corner units (Photo #3).

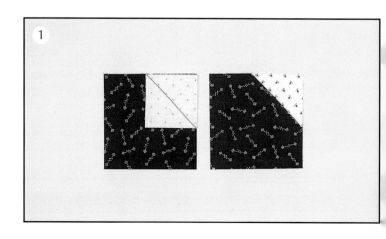

Position pieces carefully so that seams of half-square triangles are placed correctly. Press seam allowances toward squares (Photo #4).

3. Join Step 2 units, abutting seams.

Assemble the Block

1. Lay out the 4 corner units, 4 long goose units, and square E in rows as shown in Piecing Diagram.

2. Join units in 3 rows. Press seam allowances toward side units.

3. Join rows to complete the block (Photo #5).

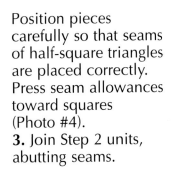

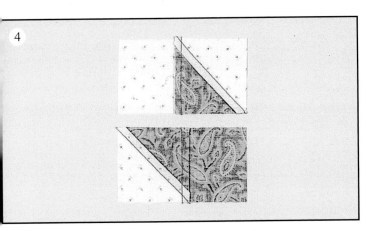

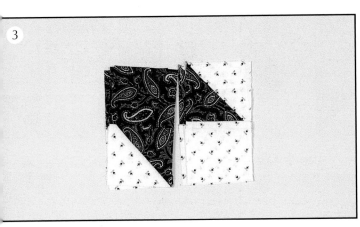

MOSAIC BLOCK
(6" finished)

The Mosaic Block introduces a new diagonal seams unit, square-in-a-square. This unit has a square turned on point in the center, surrounded by four triangles. The block also includes the now familiar goose chase units and half-square triangle units.

Cutting

From background, cut:
- 12 (2") squares for A
- 2 (2⅜") squares for C. Cut each square in half diagonally to make 4 C half-square triangles.

From 1st dark fabric, cut:
- 4 (2" x 3½") rectangles for B

From 2nd dark fabric, cut:
- 2 (2⅜") squares for C. Cut each square in half diagonally to make 4 C half-square triangles.

From 3rd dark fabric, cut:
- 1 (3½") D square

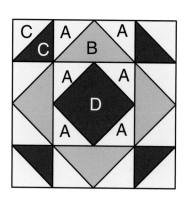

Block Diagram

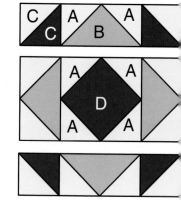

Piecing Diagram

Goose Chase Unit Diagonal Seams Diagrams

Make Square-in-a-Square Units

1. Align an A square right sides facing with opposite corners of D square. Stitch diagonally across A squares as shown in Photo #1. Open out triangles, press, and trim.

2. Align an A square with remaining two corners of D square. Stitch diagonally across A squares as shown in Photo #2. Open out triangles, press, and trim to complete square-in-a-square unit (Photo #3).

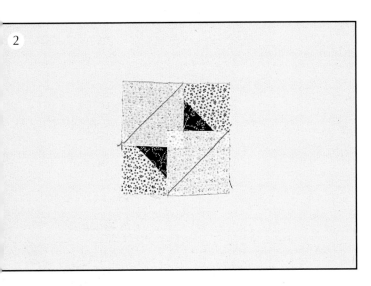

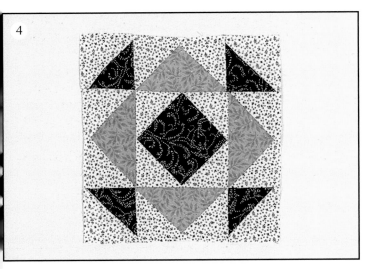

Assemble the Block

1. Referring to Goose Chase Unit Diagonal Seams Diagrams, make a goose chase unit from 2 A squares and 1 B rectangle. Repeat to make a total of 4 goose chase units.

2. Join a background C triangle to a dark C triangle to make a half-square triangle unit. Repeat to make a total of 4 half-square triangle units.

3. Lay out all units as shown in Piecing Diagram. Join units into rows. Join rows to complete block (Photo #4).

SAILBOAT BLOCK
(6" finished)

The Sailboat is a classic representational block with a masculine feel. Our quick method combines half-square triangle units and a type of diagonal seam unit that's new for you. We've affectionately named these units "flippy corner" units because diagonal seams are used just on one corner of a larger base rectangle. If you like this block a lot, make four of them for the Sail Away Wall Quilt on page 49.

Cutting
From background fabric, cut:
- 2 (2") squares for A
- 1 (2" x 3½") rectangle for D
- 1 (2¾" x 5") rectangle for E
- 1 (1¼" x 5") F rectangle
- 2 (2⅜") squares for C. Cut each square in half diagonally to make 4 C half-square triangles.

From boat fabric, cut:
- 1 (2" x 6½") rectangle for B

From sail fabric, cut:
- 2 (2") squares for A
- 2 (2⅜") squares for C. Cut each square in half diagonally to make 4 C half-square triangles.

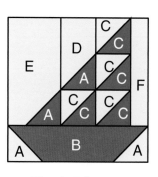

Block Diagram

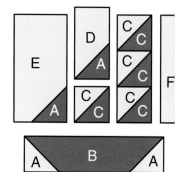

Piecing Diagram

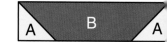

Diagonal Seams Diagrams

Make Flippy Corner Units
1. Place a sail fabric A square right sides together with lower end of D rectangle. Stitch diagonally, press, and open out as shown in Photo #1.

2. In a similar manner, add a flippy corner A square to bottom right corner of E rectangle (Photo #2).

Assemble the Block

1. Join pairs of C triangles to form 4 half-square triangle units.

2. Referring to Diagonal Seams Diagrams, use 2 A squares and 1 B rectangle to make boat unit.

3. Referring to Piecing Diagram, lay out flippy corner units, half-square triangle units, F rectangle, and boat unit. Join pieces to form vertical rows for sail unit as shown. Join rows. Join F rectangle to sail. Join boat unit to sail unit to complete block (Photo #3).

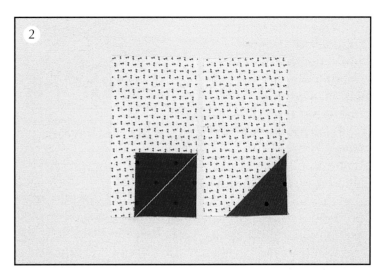

LIZ SAYS:
The Step 1 flippy corner unit is just like the beginning of a normal goose chase unit. For the boat block, though, you add only one square to form one triangle.

MARIANNE SAYS:
If you need more help, the boat unit is the same configuration as the side unit for Farmer's Daughter, page 20, the first block you made!

WHEELS BLOCK

(10" finished)

Wheels, like Jack-in-the-Box, is a directional pattern with four rotated quadrants. You'll use the diagonal seams method with a triangle as the base fabric (instead of a rectangle or square) to make a unit we call a "lopped off" triangle. When you made your Weathervane Block, you worked with half-square triangles. For Wheels, you'll also need a different type of right-angle triangle called a quarter-square triangle. See page 13 for more information on quarter-square triangles.

Cutting

From background fabric, cut:
- 1 (6¼") square for A. Cut square in quarters diagonally to make 4 A quarter-square triangles. See Quarter-Square Triangles, page 13.
- 4 (3") squares for D

From 1st dark fabric, cut:
- 1 (6¼") square for B. Cut square in quarters diagonally to make 4 B quarter-square triangles.

From 2nd dark fabric, cut:
- 2 (5⅞") squares for C. Cut each square in half diagonally (one way only!) to make a total of 4 half-square triangles for C.

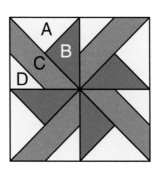

Block Diagram

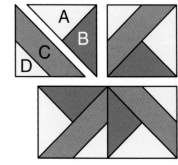

Piecing Diagram

Make the Lopped-Off Triangle Units

1. Referring to Photo #1, place 1 (3") D square atop 1 triangle C, aligning right-angle corners. Stitch diagonally.

2. Open out square to form triangle as shown in photo, check alignment, press, and trim.

3. Repeat to make a total of 4 C/D units.

Assemble the Block

1. Referring to Piecing Diagram, position A and B triangles exactly as shown. Make sure the darker B triangle is to the right of the background A triangle. Join triangles to make A/B unit.

2. Repeat to make a total of 4 identical A/B units.

3. Referring to Piecing Diagram, lay out 1 A/B unit and 1 C/D unit. Join units to form block quadrant (Photo #2). Repeat to make a total of 4 identical quadrants.
4. Lay out the 4 block quadrants, rotating each a quarter-turn. Join into 2 rows. Press seam allowances in opposite directions. Join rows, abutting seams, to complete block (Photo #3).

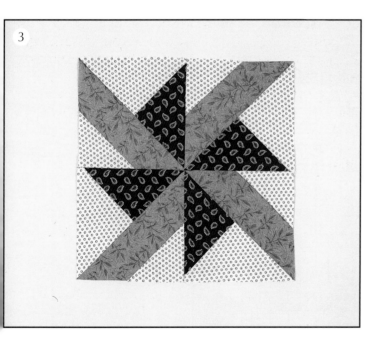

ASSEMBLE THE QUILT TOP

Join the Blocks

1. Join the Star Block to the top of the Tree Block. Add the star/tree unit to one side of the House Block to form one large block.

2. Referring to the Sampler Layout Diagrams this page, lay out your six blocks plus star/tree/house unit. You can choose a vertical or horizontal orientation for your quilt. The three 10"-finished blocks, Jack-in-the-Box, Wheels, and Farmer's Daughter, are interchangeable. The house/star/tree unit is interchangeable with the 12" Weathervane Block.

Vertical Sampler Finished size: 29" x 37"

Horizontal Sampler Finished size: 37" x 29"

3. Join the Jack-in-the-Box, Wheels, and Farmer's Daughter Blocks into a row. Press seam allowances to one side.

4. Join the Mosaic and Sailboat Blocks into a strip. Press seam allowances to one side.

5. Join the star/tree/house unit, the mosaic/sailboat unit, and the Weathervane Block into a row.

6. Join the rows.

Add the Borders

1. Measuring through the middle, rather than along the outer edge, which may be stretched, measure your quilt top. Measure the longest way first. Trim two 1"-wide borders to this size (approximately 30½", including seam allowances). Join borders to opposite sides of quilt top. Press seam allowances toward borders.

2. In a similar manner, measure the opposite direction through your quilt top. Trim two remaining 1"-wide borders to size (approximately 23½", including seam allowances). Join borders to remaining two sides. Press seam allowances toward borders.

3. Repeat Steps 1 and 2 to trim 3½"-wide borders to length and add them to quilt top. You will trim longer borders to approximately 31½" long and the shorter borders to approximately 29½" long.

Complete Your Quilt

See Making Your Quilt A Quilt, page 60, for instructions on preparing your quilt for quilting, the quilting itself, and binding.

Wisconsin quilter Debbie Challenger made her Seams Sew Fun sampler larger by adding a Stars and Trees border. For this variation, make 24 additional Star Blocks and 8 extra Tree Blocks.

Cut the inner border 1½" wide to finish 1". Join 24 Star blocks in 3 sets of 8 to make the side and top borders. Sew 1 strip to each side. Join the last strip to the top edge of the quilt. Join the 8 Tree Blocks to make the bottom border and add to quilt top. Cut outer border strips 3½" wide to finish 3".

Student Joni Delwiche of Wisconsin used fun, whimsical fabrics to make her Seams Sew Fun sampler quilt in a class taught by Marianne at Sievers School of Fiber Arts on Washington Island, WI.

Finished size: 41" x 53"
8 (6") blocks

Materials
- 1¼ yards of light fabric for blocks and setting squares
- 1¾ yards of dark fabric for blocks, borders, and binding
- 1⅝ yards of fabric for quilt back
- crib-size quilt batting (45" x 60")

Cutting
Cut all strips crosswise. Measurements include ¼" seam allowances.

From light fabric, cut:
- 7 (2½"-wide) strips for strip sets
- 3 (6½"-wide) strips. From these, cut 17 (6½") setting squares.

From dark fabric, cut:
- 8 (2½"-wide) strips for strip sets
- 4 (6½"-wide) strips for borders
- 5 (2¼"-wide) strips for binding

Make the Blocks
1. Join 2 dark strips and 1 light strip to make an A strip set as shown at top of Photo #1. Press seam allowances toward dark outer strips. Join 2 light strips and 1 dark strip to make a B strip set as shown at bottom of Photo #1. Press seam allowances toward dark center strip. Repeat to make a total of 3 A strip sets and a total of 2 B strip sets.

2. Stack several strip sets so you will be able to cut segments several at a time. When stacking, stagger strip sets about ½" as shown in Photo #2. Take care to keep strips parallel to each other.

3. Even off selvage edge of stacked strip sets by first placing your ruled square atop strip sets and aligning ruled lines with seams and raw edges. Bring edge of square close to uneven selvage edges. Abut 6" x 12" ruler against ruled square as shown in Photo #3.

4. Remove ruled square and cut off uneven edge by cutting against 6" x 12" ruler as shown in Photo #4.

5. Use ruler to cut 2½"-wide segments (Photo #5). Cut a total of 36 (2½"-wide) A strip set segments and 18 (2½"-wide) B strip set segments.

6. Referring to Piecing Diagram, page 44, join 2 A strip set segments and 1 B strip set segment to make a Nine Patch Block. Press seam allowances toward outer segments. Repeat to make a total of 18 blocks.

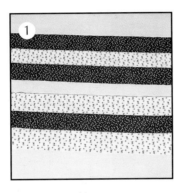
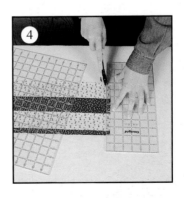
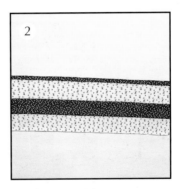

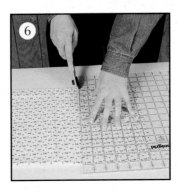

LIZ SAYS:
When cutting wide strips, use a 15" rotary cutting square to cut strips and pieces that are wider than a standard 6"-wide ruler (Photo #6)

43

Nine Patch Block

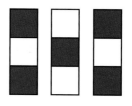

Piecing Diagram

Quilt Assembly Diagram

Assemble the Quilt

1. Referring to Quilt Assembly Diagram, join 3 Nine Patch Blocks and 2 light setting squares into a row, alternating types. Press seam allowances toward setting squares. Repeat to make a total of 4 rows of this type.

2. Join 3 light setting squares and 2 Nine Patch Blocks into a row, alternating types. Press seam allowances toward setting squares. Make a total of 3 rows of this type.

3. Join the 7 rows, alternating types and beginning and ending with Step 1 type rows. Press seam allowances to one side.

4. Measure length of quilt top and trim 2 borders to size (approximately 42½" long). Sew borders to quilt sides. Press seam allowances toward borders.

5. Measure width of quilt top, including side borders, and trim remaining borders to size (approximately 42½" long). Sew borders to top and bottom edges. Press seam allowances toward borders.

Quilting and Finishing

1. Mark quilting designs as desired. The design we used for the light setting squares is on page 68. We used a commercial quilting stencil to mark the cable design in the borders. See pages 60 - 61, for extra help with marking.

2. Layer quilt top, batting, and quilt back; baste.

3. Quilt as desired. See

QUILTER'S TIP–PIECING BORDER STRIPS FOR NEEDED LENGTH

Although most cotton fabrics for quilts are marketed as 44"-45"-wide goods, they are often narrower. If your fabric is too narrow to yield crosswise strips long enough for the borders for a small quilt, such as the Nine Patch Baby Quilt, you'll need to cut an additional 6½" wide border strip, and piece strips together to create borders the needed length. For full-size quilts such as the Row Upon Row Sampler on page 56, we cut enough crosswise strips (generally two per side) to join for the needed length.

Follow these easy steps to piece strips for borders.

1. With right sides facing, position border strips at right angles as shown in Photo A.

2. Stitch diagonally across borders as shown in Photo B. You can use the handy diagonal seams guide you have installed on your machine to make this sewing easier and more accurate.

3. Trim excess fabric to leave approximately ¼" seam allowances as shown in Photo C.

4. Working from wrong side, press seam allowances open as shown in Photo D. Turn strip over and press seam from right side.

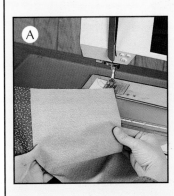

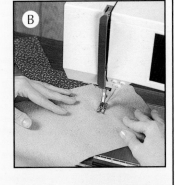

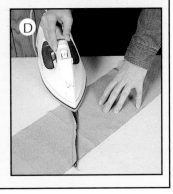

pages 62 - 64 for instructions on hand and machine quilting.

4. Following instructions on pages 65 - 67, make French-fold binding from dark fabric strips. Finish edges of quilt with binding.

LIZ SAYS: See Making Your Quilt A Quilt on page 60 for instructions on marking designs as well as on layering, quilting, and binding your quilt.

Finished size: 24" x 26"

Materials
- 1 yard of tan print for backgrounds and quilt back
- *Fat eighth yard of green print for trees
- Fat eighth yard of red and tan check for trees and house
- ½ yard of red print for house and binding
- Fat eighth yard of light gold print for stars
- Fat eighth yard of dark gold print for stars and house
- Fat eighth yard of black print for house
- ⅜ yard of black stripe for borders
- 27" x 29" rectangle of quilt batting

*Fat eighth yard = 9" x 21"

Cutting
Cut strips across the fabric width. Measurements for all pieces include ¼" seam allowances.

Letters in cutting instructions correspond to piecing instructions for each block in the quilt (Tree, and Star, and House, pages 22, 24, and 28).

From tan fabric, cut:
- 1 (27" x 29") rectangle for quilt back

Trees:
- 2 (2½" x 42") strips. From these, cut 24 (2½") squares for A and 4 (2" x 2½") C rectangles for trunk unit.
  House:
- 1 (4½") square for A
- 1 (2½" x 4½") rectangle for B
- 1 (1½" x 4½") rectangle for D
- 1 (2½" x 8½") rectangle for spacer at top of house
  Stars:
- 16 (1½") C squares
- 16 (1½" x 2½") rectangles for B

From green print fabric, cut:
  Trees:
- 3 (2½" x 21") strips. From these, cut 12 (2½" x 4½") rectangles for B.

From red and tan check fabric, cut:
  Trees:
- 2 (1½" x 2½") D rectangles (trunk)
  House:
- 1 (2½" x 6½") J rectangle (door)
- 1 (1½" x 4½") rectangle for C (chimney)

From red print fabric, cut:
- 3 (2¼" x 42") strips for binding
- 1 (4½" x 42") strip. From this, cut 4 (4½") squares for border corners.

From remaining 4½"-wide red print fabric strip, cut:
  House:
- 1 (4½" x 8½") rectangle for E (roof)

From light gold fabric, cut:
  Stars:
- 1 (2½" x 21") strip. From this, cut 4 (2½") D squares.

From dark gold fabric, cut:
  Stars:
- 3 (1½" x 21") strips. From these, cut 32 (1½") squares for A.
  House:
- 1 (2½" x 3½") H rectangle (window)

From black print fabric, cut:
  House:
- 1 (2½" x 21") strip. From this, cut 1 (2½" x 8½") F rectangle, 1 (2½" x 6½") K rectangle, and 1 (2½" x 3½") G rectangle.
- 1 (1½" x 21") strip. From this, cut 2 (1½" x 6½") I rectangles.

From black stripe fabric, cut:
- 2 (4½" x 42") strips. From these, cut 2 (4½" x 16½") rectangles for top and bottom borders and 2 (4½" x 18½") rectangles for side borders.

LIZ SAYS:
When you're cutting a variety of sizes and shapes for a quilt project, cut biggest pieces first; then, cut smaller pieces for patchwork from your leftovers.

Piecing

1. Following instructions on pages 28 - 29, make 1 House Block. Add the 2½" x 8½" tan rectangle to top edge of house. Press seam allowance toward rectangle.

2. Following instructions on pages 22 - 23, make 12 A/B goose chase units for tree tops and 2 C/D units for trunk sections. Join 6 A/B units to form tree. Add trunk unit to bottom edge to complete tall tree. Repeat to make a second tree. Referring to Quilt Assembly Diagram, add trees to sides of house. Press seam allowances toward house.

3. Following instructions on page 24, make 4 stars. Join 4 stars into a row. Join star row to top of tree/house unit. Press seam allowances toward tree/house unit.

4. Sew 18½"-long borders to opposite sides. Press seam allowances toward borders. Add 4½" red print squares to both ends of 16½"-long borders. Press seam allowances toward borders. Add borders to top and bottom edges of quilt top.

Quilting and Finishing

1. Layer quilt top, batting, and quilt back; baste.

2. Quilt as desired. See pages 62 - 64 for instructions on hand and machine quilting.

3. Following instructions on pages 65 - 67, make French-fold binding from red print strips. Finish edges of quilt with binding.

Quilt Assembly Diagram

Quilt Top Diagram

Finished size:
22½" x 22½"
Four 6" Sailboat Blocks

Materials
- ¾ yard of cream print for sails, pinwheels, and quilt back
- ½ yard of red print for boats, borders, and binding
- ½ yard of blue print for boat backgrounds and spacers
- 27" x 27" square of quilt batting

Cutting
Cut strips across fabric width. Measurements include ¼" seam allowances.

Letters in cutting instructions correspond to piecing instructions for Sailboat Block, page 36.

From cream fabric, cut:
- 1 (27") square (quilt back)
- 2 (2" x 13") strips. From these, cut 8 (2") squares for A (sails).
- 4 (2⅜" x 13") strips. From these, cut 16 (2⅜") squares. Cut squares in half diagonally to make 32 C triangles (16 for sails and 16 for pinwheels).

From blue fabric, cut:
- 4 (2"-wide) strips. From these, cut:
- 3 (2" x 17") rectangles (horizontal spacers)
- 4 (2" x 3½") rectangles for D
- 8 (2") squares for A
- 6 (2" x 6½") rectangles (vertical spacers)

- 1 (2⅜"-wide) strip. From this, cut 16 (2⅜") squares. Cut squares in half diagonally to make 32 C triangles (16 for sail units and 16 for pinwheels).
- 1 (5"-wide) strip. From this, cut:
- 4 (2¾" x 5") rectangles for E
- 4 (1¼" x 5") F rectangles

From red print, cut:
- 1 (2"-wide) strip. From this, cut 4 (2" x 6½") rectangles for B (boats)
- 2 (3½"-wide) strips. From these, cut 4 (3½" x 17") rectangles for borders
- 3 (2¼"-wide) strips for binding

Piecing
1. Following instructions on pages 36 - 37, make 4 Sailboat Blocks.
2. Referring to Quilt Assembly Diagram, join 3 vertical spacer strips and 2 Sailboat Blocks into a row, alternating types of pieces. Press seam allowances toward spacer strips. Repeat to make a second row.
3. Join 3 horizontal spacer strips and sailboat rows, alternating types of pieces. Press seam allowances toward spacer strips.
4. Join remaining blue and white A triangles to make 16 half-square triangle units. Lay out 4 units as shown in Pinwheel Piecing Diagram. Join units into pairs; join pairs to make Pinwheel. Repeat to make 4 Pinwheel Blocks.
5. Sew borders to opposite sides of quilt top. Press seam allowances toward borders. Join a Pinwheel to each end of remaining borders. Press seam allowances toward borders. Add borders to top and bottom edges. Press seam allowances toward borders.

Quilting and Finishing
1. Layer quilt top, batting, and quilt back; baste.
2. Quilt as desired. See pages 62 - 64 for instructions on hand and machine quilting.
3. Following instructions on pages 65 - 67, make French-fold binding from red print strips. Finish edges of quilt with binding.

MARIANNE SAYS:
Cut quilt back first; then, use remaining fabric to cut strips for smaller pieces.

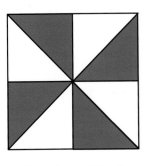

Pinwheel Block

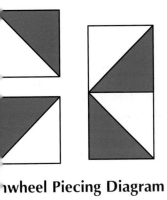

Pinwheel Piecing Diagram

Quilt Assembly Diagram

Quilt Top Diagram

Finished size:
60½" x 48½"

Three 10" Wheels Blocks

Materials

- 1½ yards of white-and-yellow print fabric for quilt back and patchwork blocks
- *Fat quarter of blue print
- 1 yard of yellow print for blocks, borders, and binding
- ½ yard of blue-and-yellow print for setting triangles
- 24" x 54" rectangle of batting

Fat quarter =18" x 21".

Cutting

Cut strips across fabric width unless directed otherwise. Measurements include ¼" seam allowances.

Letters in cutting instructions correspond to piecing instructions for Wheels Block, page 38.

From white-and-yellow print, cut:
- 1 *lengthwise* piece, 24" wide by 54" long, for quilt back.

From remaining fabric, cut:
- 3 (6¼") squares for A. Cut each square in quarters diagonally to make 12 A triangles.
- 12 (3") squares for D.

From blue print, cut:
- 2 (5⅞" x 21") strips. From these, cut 6 (5⅞") squares for C. Cut each square in half diagonally to make 12 half-square triangles for C.

From yellow print, cut:
- 4 (3½"-wide) strips for borders
- 4 (2¼"-wide) strips for binding
- 1 (6¼"-wide) strip. From strip cut 3 (6¼") squares for A. Cut each square in quarters diagonally to make 12 A triangles.

From blue-and-yellow print, cut:
- 1 (16") square. Cut square in quarters diagonally to make 4 X side setting triangles.
- 2 (9") squares. Cut each square in half diagonally to make 4 Y corner setting triangles.

Piecing

1. Following instructions on pages 38 - 39, make 3 Wheels Blocks.
2. Referring to Row Assembly Diagram #1, page 54, lay out 3 Wheels Blocks, 4 X setting triangles, and 4 Y corner setting triangles as shown.
3. Join blocks and setting triangles in diagonal rows as shown. Match square corners of X setting triangles to corners of blocks. (Excess at points of triangles will extend beyond blocks.) Fold Y triangles in half to determine center. Match centers of Y triangles to centers of sides of blocks. (Excess at points of triangles will extend beyond blocks.)

MARIANNE SAYS:
If your cutting mat is marked in a grid of 1" squares, you can use the grid as a guide to cut the large 16" square. An alternate method is to use your large rotary cutting square and a ruler together to measure and cut these large squares.

LIZ SAYS:
The X side setting triangles are cut as quarter-square triangles so that the hypotenuse, longest side, is on the fabric straight of grain. The Y corner setting triangles are cut as half-square triangles so that the legs, short sides, are on the fabric straight of grain. Cutting the pieces in this way places the fabric straight of grain along the outer edge of the table runner. This will make it less likely to stretch out of shape.

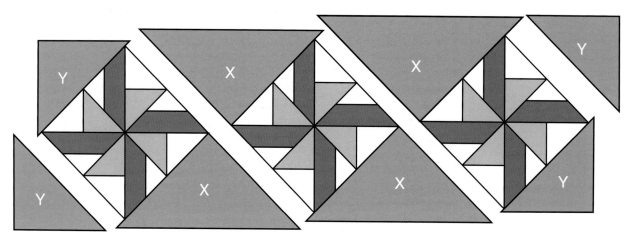

Row Assembly Diagram #1

LIZ SAYS:
Allowing ¹⁄₂" seam allowances beyond the corners of the blocks will make your blocks "float" a bit (not touch the borders). If you were to allow only ¹⁄₄" seam allowances beyond the block corners, the blocks would meet the edge of the borders. Floating the blocks is sometimes easier than having them meet the borders exactly.

MARIANNE SAYS:
Always measure for borders by measuring through the center of the quilt, rather than along the edges. Edges tend to stretch. If you use an edge measurement, you are likely to wind up with "ruffled" borders!

4. Join diagonal rows. Use a 24" long ruler to trim sides of triangles so they extend ¹⁄₂" beyond corners of blocks. Use large square to check that corners of project are true. ***Note from Marianne:*** We instructed you to cut the side and corner setting triangles slightly larger than needed to make assembling the pieces easier. You'll trim the excess later.

5. Measure length of project. Trim 2 borders to this length (approximately 42" long). Sew borders to long sides of project. Press seam allowances toward borders. Measure width of project, including borders, and trim remaining 2 borders to this length (approximately 21" long). Sew borders to ends of project. Press seam allowances toward borders.

Quilting and Finishing
1. Layer quilt top, batting, and quilt back; baste.
2. Quilt as desired. See pages 62 - 64 for instructions for hand and machine quilting.
3. Following instruction on pages 65 - 67, make French-fold binding from yellow print strips Finish edges of quilt with binding.

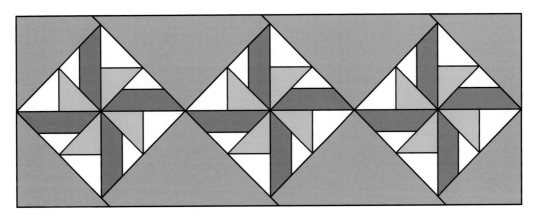

Row Assembly Diagram #2

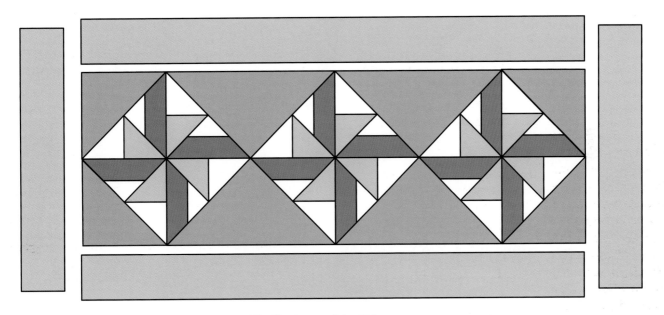

Quilt Assembly Diagram

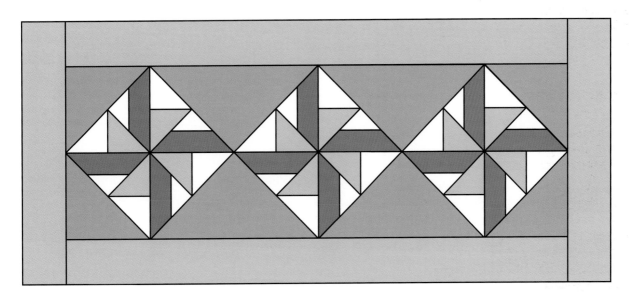

Quilt Top Diagram

Finished Size: 75" x 93"

Materials

Note: Colors in parentheses indicate colors we used for our quilt, pictured on page 56. Substitute different colors as you wish to make your own quilt.

- 3 yards of dark print fabric (navy) for outer borders, binding, and patchwork
- 1 yard of medium print (pink) fabric for inner borders and patchwork
- 1 yard each of 4-5 light background fabrics
- ½ yard each of 5-6 light prints ("shirtings") for block backgrounds
- ½ yard each of 16-18 medium to dark print fabrics (We used 4 red, 4 blue, 3 green, 3 gold, 1 black, and 1 brown. We also used the navy and pink border prints in the patchwork blocks.)
- 5½ yards fabric for quilt back

Cutting

Cut all strips crosswise. Measurements include ¼" seam allowances. Cut pieces for individual blocks by referring to cutting instructions included with each block lesson (pages 20 - 39). Cut enough pieces to make the number of blocks required for each row.

From dark print border fabric, cut:
- 8 (6½"-wide) strips for outer borders
- 9 (2¼"-wide) strips for binding

From medium print border fabric, cut:
- 8 (2"-wide) strips for inner borders

From 6 dark fabrics, cut:
- 2 (2½"-wide) strips from each fabric for spacer strips

Note: After you have cut these large pieces, use leftover fabric to cut pieces for patchwork blocks.

Make the Rows

Wheels Row
Refer to Lesson #9, page 38
1. Cut pieces for 6 Wheels Blocks.
2. Piece 6 Wheels Blocks. Join blocks together to make a row.

Mosaic Row
Refer to Lesson #7, page 34
1. Cut pieces for 10 Mosaic Blocks.
2. Piece 10 Mosaic Blocks. Join blocks together to make a row.

Farmer's Daughter Row
Refer to Lesson #1, page 20
1. Cut pieces for 6 Farmer's Daughter Blocks.
2. Piece 6 Farmer's Daughter Blocks. Join blocks together to make a row.

Sailboat Row
Refer to Lesson #8, page 36
1. Cut pieces for 10 Sailboat Blocks.
2. Piece 10 Sailboat Blocks. Join blocks together to make a row.

Jack-in-the-Box Row
Refer to Lesson #5, page 30
1. Cut pieces for 6 Jack-in-the-Box Blocks.
2. Piece 6 Jack-in-the-Box Blocks. Join blocks together to make a row.

Tree/Star/House Row
Refer to Lessons #2, #3, and #4, pages 22, 24, and 28
1. Cut pieces for 5 House Blocks, 5 Star Blocks, and 5 Tree Blocks.
2. Piece 5 blocks of each type.
3. Sew Star Block to top of Tree Block. Join star/tree unit to side of House Block.
4. Repeat to make a total of 5 house/star/tree units. Join units to make row.

Weathervane Row
Refer to Lesson #6, page 32
1. Cut pieces for 5 Weathervane Blocks.
2. Piece 5 Weathervane Blocks. Join blocks together to make a row.

MARIANNE SAYS: I used light-colored fabrics called "shirtings" for the background areas of our Row Upon Row quilt. Shirtings are regular, broadcloth-weight cotton fabrics that are white or off-white and have tiny dark motifs. These fabrics were very popular with American quilters in the 19th century and give a new quilt an old-fashioned look. Some of my shirtings are darker than others. Alternating the value of block backgrounds helps the individual blocks show up.

LIZ SAYS: One of the great things about scrap quilts is you don't have to worry about running out of fabrics. You can always add a little bit of a similar print if you see you are running out of something.

Join the Rows

1. Refer to Piecing Border Strips for Needed Length on page 45 and join pairs of matching 2½"-wide spacer strips to make 6 (60½"-long) spacer strips.

2. Referring to Quilt Assembly Diagram, join rows and spacer strips.

3. Join pairs of 2"-wide border strips to make 4 borders. Measure length of quilt; trim 2 border strips to this length. Fold border in half widthwise and crease lightly to form center guideline. Fold quilt top in half widthwise and place a pin at halfway point. Matching guideline and pin, as well as ends of border strips and quilt top, join 1 side border to quilt top. Press seam allowances toward border strip. Repeat for opposite side. In the same manner, measure and add top and bottom borders.

4. Choose light fabrics and dark fabrics for each of the 4 Pinwheel border corner blocks. From each fabric, cut 2 (3⅞") squares. Cut each square in half diagonally to make 4 half-square triangles. Cut enough triangles so you have 4 light and 4 dark for each block.

5. Refer to Pinwheel Piecing Diagram, and join 1 light and 1 dark half square triangle to make a half-square triangle unit. Repeat to make a total of 4 half-square triangle units.

6. Join 4 half-square triangle units to make a Pinwheel corner block. Repeat to make 4 blocks.

7. Measure quilt length and width. Trim 2 outer borders to measurement of quilt length and 2 to quilt width. Join longer borders to opposite sides of quilt top. Press seam allowances toward borders.

8. Join Pinwheel corner blocks to opposite ends of remaining borders. Press seam allowances toward borders. Join borders to top and bottom edges of quilt top.

Quilting and Finishing

1. Divide backing fabric into 2 (2¾-yard) panels. Cut 1 panel in half lengthwise. Join half panels to sides of wide panel.

2. Mark desired quilting designs on quilt top. See pages 60 - 61 for extra help with marking.

3. Layer quilt top, batting, and quilt back; baste.

4. Quilt as desired. See pages 62 - 64 for instructions on hand and machine quilting.

5. Following instructions on pages 65 - 67, make French-fold binding from dark print strips. Finish edges of quilt with binding.

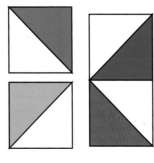

Piecing Diagram

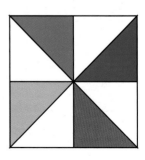

Pinwheel Block

Row Upon Row Sampler 60" x 78" (without borders)

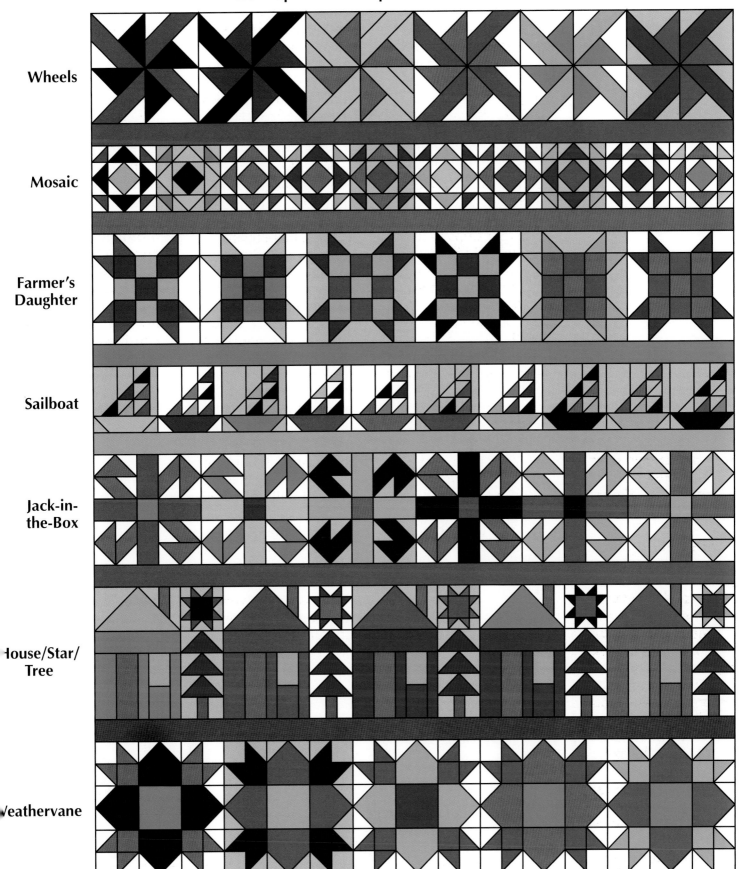

Wheels

Mosaic

Farmer's
Daughter

Sailboat

Jack-in-
the-Box

House/Star/
Tree

Weathervane

Quilt Assembly Diagram

MAKING YOUR QUILT A QUILT

Once you've pieced your blocks and joined them into a quilt top, you're ready for the exciting final stages of a project—the steps that make it a quilt. These guidelines will help you with all your beginning projects.

You'll need a few extra supplies, which we'll mention in the sections below. Some of them are optional, depending on what kind of quilting designs and the type of quilting you choose.

GET READY TO QUILT
Marking Quilting Designs
Additional supplies:
• marking pencils
• quilt design stencils
• freezer paper
• tracing paper
• permanent marker
• large needle

MARIANNE SAYS:
Before using any marker on a quilt top, test to make sure the marks will wash out of the fabric. Mark on fabric scraps from the quilt and wash them in the sink or in the washer with other laundry.

If quilting must be marked, do the marking before basting layers for quilting. Commercial quilting stencils are available in many different designs and are handy for marking intricate designs on any fabric (Photo #1).

To mark a quilting design from a printed pattern, trace it onto freezer paper. Darken lines with a permanent marker.

For fabrics light enough to see through, position the paper pattern under the quilt top and trace lines neatly onto fabric with a washable pencil such as an artist's silver pencil. For dark fabrics that you can't see through easily, use a large needle to punch holes in the paper pattern. With the pattern atop the quilt, mark through the holes, making small dots on the quilt top (Photo #2).

Making the Quilt Back
For the projects in this book, we have included the amount o 45"-wide fabric you will need for the quilt back in the materials list. Backing for small projects like the Seams Sew Fun sampler quilt and others is easily made from a single width of fabric. For a full-size quilt like the Row Upon Row sampler, you'll need to piece a larger backing. The project instruction tell you how to divide the backing fabric and construct the quilt back.

Batting
We favor low-loft battings for our quilts. We like the flat, old-fashioned look that cotton or cotton/polyester batting gives. Batting manufacturers have made great improvements in their cotton products, and the new cotton and cotton blen battings do not require the very close quilting that cotton battings of the past did. Read the manufacturer's information on the package carefully before you use a brand of batting in your quilt.

Although cotton battings are somewhat more difficult to hand quilt than polyester battings, cotton is the batting of choice for most machine quilters. Its reduced bulk makes a large quilt more manageable for machine quilting. Also, the quilt top and quilt back tend to cling to the cotton battings, reducing the chances of puckers or pleats.

Before layering and basting your quilt, unwrap and unfold the batting and let it breathe for a few hours to relax creases. You can tumble dry stable types of batts on low heat for three to five minutes to relax them.

Choosing Hand or Machine Quilting

We make our decision on whether to hand or machine quilt before we layer and baste our quilts because we use different basting methods depending on the quilting method we will be using. All of the projects in this book were machine quilted.

Layering a Quilt

Choose a large work surface where you can spread out the quilt—a large table, two tables pushed together, or a clean hard surface or carpeted floor.

Fold the backing in half lengthwise and lightly crease to create a center guideline. Fold batting and quilt top in half and use straight pins to mark center guidelines.

Lay the quilt back out wrong side up on the work surface. Secure one long side of the quilt back to the work surface with masking tape or T-pins if working on carpet.

Move to the opposite side of the quilt back. Gently tug on the quilt back to remove any wrinkles or folds and tape or pin edge to work surface. Repeat for the two short ends. The back should be taut but not stretched out of shape.

Matching center marks, place batting on quilt back and smooth out any wrinkles or

excess fullness. Center and place quilt top on batting. Again, smooth out any wrinkles or fullness. Layers must be smooth, and batting and backing should be two to three inches larger than quilt top on all sides.

Thread Basting

Additional supplies:
• light colored cotton thread
• long darning needle

Using light colored thread and a long hand sewing needle, begin basting at the center of the quilt and work toward the outside edges. Baste with a horizontal tailor's padding stitch, basting the quilt every four to six inches (Photo #3).

If you plan to use a hoop for quilting, roll the backing and batting over on outside edges and baste to protect batting from tearing during quilting. Follow

manufacturer's instructions if you are putting the quilt in a floor frame.

Safety Pin Basting

Additional supplies:
• rustproof safety pins (500 to 700 1"-long pins for a full-size quilt)
• Quick Clip (optional)
• Quilt Tak (optional)

Pin the layers together with 1"-long brass or nickel-plated safety pins, beginning at the center of the quilt and working toward the outer edges. Place a pin approximately every three to four inches. Check spacing by placing your fist randomly on the quilt top—the edges of your fist should always touch pins. Work entirely from the quilt top, pinning through all three layers, without reaching under the quilt.

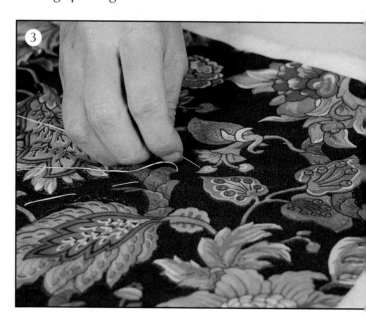

62

QUILTING
Hand Quilting

Additional supplies:
"betweens" quilting
   needles, size 7 or 8
14" quilting hoop
thimble
quilting thread
scissors

Hand quilting stitches should be evenly spaced, with the spaces between stitches about the same length as the stitches themselves. Stitches should look similar on quilt top and back. The number of stitches per inch is less important than the uniformity of the stitching.

1. Start by placing your work in a frame or hoop. Sit in a comfortable chair near good light. Have your thimble, scissors, thread, and quilting needles at hand. Position yourself so that the line of quilting angles from upper right to lower left, so that you can quilt toward yourself. (Reverse directions if you are left-handed.)

2. Use a short needle called a "between." If you are a beginner, try a size 7 or 8. As your skill increases, a smaller (shorter) needle will help you make smaller stitches. Thread the needle with an 18"-24" length of quilting thread and make a small knot in the cut end.

3. Insert the needle through the quilt top, about one inch from the position where you want to begin. Slide the needle through the batting, without piercing the backing. Bring the needle up at the beginning point and pull the thread until the knot stops on the surface of the fabric. Tug the thread gently to pop the knot through the top into the batting. Use a thumbnail to encourage the knot in through the threads.

4. Place your non-sewing hand under the quilt. Insert the needle with the point straight down as shown in Photo #4, about $\frac{1}{16}$" from where the thread comes up. With your underneath finger, feel for the point of the needle as it comes through the backing. With practice, you will be able to find the point without pricking your finger.

5. Push the fabric up from below as you rock the needle to a nearly horizontal position.

Using the thumb of your sewing hand as shown in Photo #5 and the underneath hand, form a little hill in the fabric and push the tip of the needle back through the quilt top.

6. Rock the needle to an upright position to take another stitch before pulling it through. At first, load only two or three stitches on the needle. As you gain experience, try loading a few more stitches at one time.

7. End the line of quilting when you have about six inches of thread left. Tie a knot in the thread close to the quilt surface. Pop the knot through the top as before, and clip the tail. Rethread the needle and continue quilting.

Machine Quilting
Additional supplies:
- even-feed presser foot or walking foot for straight line quilting
- sewing machine that allows you to either drop the feed dogs or cover them with a special plate for free-motion quilting

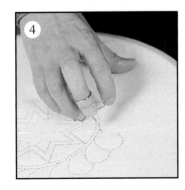

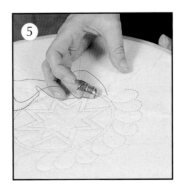

LIZ SAYS:
The smaller the number of a hand sewing needle, the larger the needle. For example, size 7 "betweens" are much larger than size 10 "betweens." Machine sewing needles are sized just the opposite. The smaller the number of the sewing machine needle, the smaller the needle.

- darning or ring-type presser foot for free-motion quilting
- top thread—size .004 monofilament nylon thread OR regular sewing thread or machine embroidery thread in a color that blends with the fabrics in the quilt
- bobbin thread—regular sewing thread in a color that blends with the quilt back fabric
- bicycle clips or machine quilting clips to keep the quilt rolled up while working

Preparing for Machine Quilting:

Adjust the tension so the bottom thread is not pulled to the top. Usually you will need to loosen the top tension slightly or thread your bobbin thread through a hole in the bobbin case. Set needle to stop in down position or try to stop stitching with needle in fabric.

Roll and fold the quilt if machine quilting a large quilt. Secure rolls with bicycle clips. Some quilters prefer to leave the quilt open and sling the quilt over their shoulder or hold it on their lap.

Extend your sewing machine work area by setting up tables to the left and behind your machine to help support a large quilt while you are working.

MARIANNE SAYS: Sewing machine needles specially designed for machine quilting have sharp points and reduce the incidents of skipped stitches.

Beginning and Ending Machine Quilting:

Turn the hand wheel to take a stitch, pulling on the top thread to bring the bobbin thread to the surface (Photo #6). Hold onto both threads to prevent them from tangling when you begin quilting.

To secure ends of threads at beginning and end of lines of stitching, make very tiny, close stitches for approximately ¼-inch.

Quilting Straight Lines:

1. Attach a walking foot to your machine and adjust the stitch length to approximately 6 to 10 stitches per inch, or between 3 and 3.5 on some machines.

2. As you quilt, use your hands to assist the walking foot. Spread the fabric slightly with your hands and gently push fabric toward the walking foot to prevent puckering and reduce the drag on the fabrics (Photo #7).

Free-Motion Quilting:

Free-motion machine quilting is a skill most of us must practice in order to master. On your first attempts, keep your projects small so they are easier to manipulate. At first, concentrate on following the design; smooth, even stitches will come with practice. Do not become discouraged if your first attempts are less than perfect.

1. Attach a darning foot or free-motion quilting foot and lower the feed dogs or cover them. No stitch length adjustment is necessary; you will control the stitch length by manually moving the fabric.

2. Rest fingertips on fabric, with a hand on each side of presser foot so you can move the fabric freely and evenly. To make even stitches, run the machine at a steady, medium speed and move the fabric smoothly and evenly so that the needle follows the design (Photo #8). Do not rotate quilt; simply move the fabric forward, backward, and side to side.

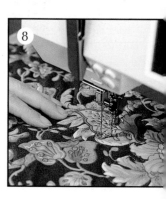

BINDING
Making French-fold Binding (Straight Grain)

We use straight grain binding to finish our quilts. Bias binding is only necessary for quilts with curved outer edges.

1. Cut sufficient number of fabric strips across the width of the fabric to join into a strip the length needed to bind the quilt. For the projects in this book, the instructions tell you how many strips you need. We generally cut strips 2¼" inches wide because we like low-loft cotton battings.

2. Join strips end-to-end to make a continuous strip. To join strips, position ends perpendicular to each other with right sides facing. Stitch across strips as shown in Photo #9 to make a diagonal seam. Trim to ¼-inch seam allowances; press seam allowances open.

3. Fold binding in half along the length of the strip and press fold (Photo #10).

Attaching Binding and Mitering Corners

Additional supplies:
- pencil
- small ruled square with 45° angle line

Binding is sewn to the front of the quilt first, then turned and finished on the back, covering raw edges.

1. Begin sewing on binding along middle of any quilt side. Leave about a 12" tail unstitched before you begin stitching binding to the quilt. Align raw edges of binding with edge of quilt top and stitch through all layers using a ¼-inch-wide seam.

2. To miter corners, stop stitching ¼-inch from quilt corner, backstitch, and remove quilt from sewing machine (Photo #11). Placing a pin at ¼-inch point will help you know where to stop stitching.

3. Rotate quilt a quarter turn. Fold binding straight up, away from corner, forming a 45°-angle fold (Photo #12, page 66).

4. Bring binding straight down in line with next edge to be sewn, leaving top fold even with the raw edge of previously sewn side. Begin stitching at top edge, sewing through all layers (Photo #13, page 66). Repeat for all four corners.

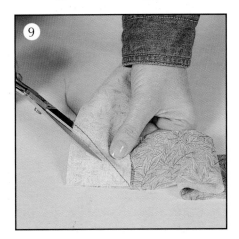

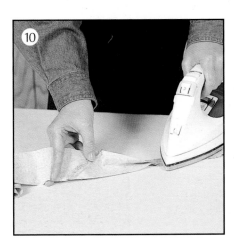

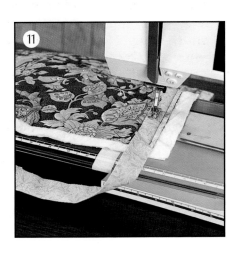

MARIANNE SAYS:
Using a walking foot when machine stitching binding helps prevent puckers from forming as you stitch. If you don't have a walking foot, hand baste around edge of quilt to keep layers from shifting when you sew on the binding.

5. Stop stitching about 8" away from starting point. Bring beginning and end of binding to center of 8" opening and fold each back, leaving about 1/4" space between the two folds of binding as shown in Photo #14.

6. Open out each end of binding and draw a line across the wrong side of the binding in the width-wise fold line, as shown in Photo #15. Draw a line through the lengthwise fold of the binding at the same spot to create an X.

7. With the edge of the ruler at the marked X, line up the 45°-angle marking on a ruler with one long side of the binding. Draw a diagonal line across the binding as shown in Photo #16.

8. Repeat for the other end of the binding. The lines must angle in the same direction (Photo #17).

9. Pin binding ends with right sides facing, pin-matching diagonal lines as shown in Photo #18. Binding ends will be at right angles to each other.

10. Keeping binding away from quilt, machine-stitch along diagonal line, removing pins as you stitch (Photo #19).

11. Lay binding against the quilt edge to double check that it is the correct length. Trim ends of binding 1/4" from the diagonal seam (Photo #20).

LIZ SAYS:
Allowing 1/4" space is critical. The binding tends to stretch as you stitch it to the quilt. If folded ends meet at this point, the binding will be too long for the space after the ends are joined.

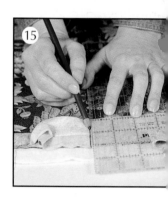

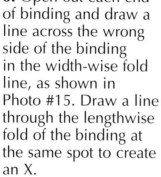
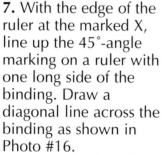
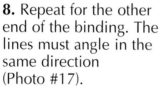
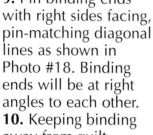

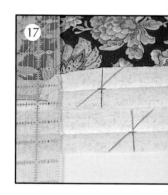
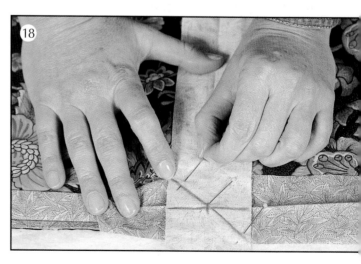

2. Finger-press [di]agonal seam open [P]hoto #21). Fold the [bi]nding in half and [fi]nish stitching the [bi]nding to the quilt.
3. Trim excess batting [an]d quilt back, leaving [en]ough to fill binding [fir]mly.
4. Turn binding over [se]am allowance to quilt [ba]ck. Blind stitch fold [of] backing fabric as [sh]own in Photo #22.
5. At corners, fold [bi]nding to miter and [bl]indstitch along [di]agonal fold [P]hoto #23).

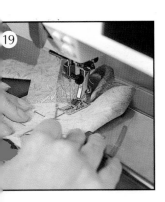

SIGNING YOUR QUILT
Additional supplies:
- muslin scraps
- freezer paper
- permanent fabric marking pens

Signing and dating your work is an important step in finishing a quilt. Sometimes we like to add additional information such as the occasion for which the quilt was made, the length of time it took to make the quilt, and the recipient of the quilt.

Cut a square of muslin and a matching size square of plastic-coated freezer paper the size you want your signature patch to be. Using a dry iron set at wool, adhere the shiny side of the freezer paper to the muslin to stabilize fabric while writing.

Use a fine-tip permanent marking pen, such as a Pilot Scuff™ or Micron Pigma™, to write on the muslin. Peel off freezer paper. Turn under seam allowances around the patch. Hand blind stitch the patch to the quilt back.

MAKING AND ADDING A HANGING SLEEVE
Wall quilts and large quilts that are hung for display often have a sleeve on the back through which you can insert a pole.
1. From extra quilt back fabric or muslin, cut a 8½-inch-wide fabric piece that measures the width of the quilt, piecing shorter strips as needed to achieve length.
2. Turn in one inch to wrong side twice on ends of strips and machine hem. With wrong sides facing, join long edges. Press the seam allowances open, centering the seam on one side of the tube.
3. With the seam facing the quilt back, place the sleeve just below the binding at the top of the quilt, centering it between the sides. Blind stitch the top and bottom edges of the sleeve to the quilt back only, making sure no stitches go through to the quilt top.

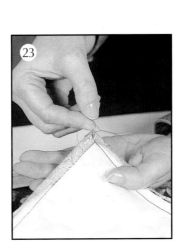

MARIANNE SAYS:
When we trim away excess batting and quilt back, we like to trim so that a scant 1/8" of batting and backing extends beyond the raw edges of the binding. This ensures a nicely "filled" binding.

LIZ SAYS:
Think of the signature patch as a diary of the history of your quilt.

**Quilting Design for
Nine Patch Baby Quilt**

Kits are available for some of the projects shown in this book.
For information, call
Fons and Porter Quilt Supply, 1-888-985-1020,
or visit our web site at fonsandporter.com

Bernina sewing machine and iron provided by Sew Smart, Inc.,
Little Rock, Arkansas

We appreciate Cabin Fever and Antique Mall, Mayflower, Arkansas,
for allowing us to photograph the Nine Patch Baby Quilt in their shop.

Production Team:
Art - Rhonda Shelby
Editing - Beth Knife, Heather Doyal